Racing DEATH

A Radical Pursuit

Daniel K. O'Neill

Printed in Canada

ISBN: 978-1-4866-1464-6

Word Alive Press
119 De Baets Street Winnipeg, MB R2J 3R9
www.wordalivepress.ca

Library and Archives Canada Cataloguing in Publication

O'Neill, Daniel K., 1963-, author
    Racing death : a radical pursuit / Daniel K. O'Neill.

Issued in print and electronic formats.
ISBN 978-1-4866-1464-6 (softcover).--ISBN 978-1-4866-1465-3 (ebook)

    1. Christian life. I. Title.

BV4501.3.O5827 2017   248.4   C2017-902547-3
                                             C2017-902548-1

In memory of Garrett Markiwsky.

We travelled the path together for a short time.
You will always remain with me.
Thank you for being a great friend.

CONTENTS

ABOUT DANIEL

"Live remarkably and follow the spirit in your heart."

Man, I love that tag line. I came up with it for my book, *Nobody Can Take It Away from You*. That line found me and carried me along the path to where I am in my life now. I am an author, athlete, and coach. I live my life from the inside out, not following the societal model that lives from the outside in. I am unapologetically weird. The status quo leads to mediocrity, and I'm not going to be mediocre. My tank is fuelled by a different means of energy that is renewable, relevant, and always present. I'm talking about the Holy Spirit—the great gift we received when Jesus rose again to allow us to pursue life eternal.

My path hasn't always been smooth or focused. As a young boy I was sexually abused by a priest, which massively impacted my relationship with God. I tried to run as far away from God as I could, but He's a much better runner than I'll ever be. Anger in my youth developed in me a mindset in which I couldn't separate God from the church … until God showed me that there's a massive difference between the two. No offence to any church … I just dig living with God by a different means.

I enjoy the endurance aspect of life. Life is energy, bold, brilliant, and abundant. I like to step out into that energy and ride the wave with passion and perseverance. I've learned a thing or two about grit and discipline on my journey. I believe that there's nothing we can't accomplish when we live in harmony with the energy of God. As an endurance athlete, I will continue to push the limits of my physical endurance, because when I come out the other side, I am living in Spirit.

My objective is to inspire and motivate others as they journey along their path. One of the greatest rewards I get from coaching is witnessing another person achieve their objective. We are designed to thrive, not decay. I pursue life in a way that allows me to interact with, train with, and race with other amazing people. I've learned great lessons from those people and my own endeavours that I use to help others rise above societal conditioning. We can strip away the limits we put on ourselves and move the needle in a positive way.

In order to achieve my own objectives, I've had to be unreasonable in my pursuit of a life that allows me to be fully alive. I live an unconventional life to create the energy, mindset, and attitude I want so that my days are dictated by my relationship with God and pursuing His Vision for me. I have developed a philosophy that I've labelled UN. We're able to create incredible abundance in our lives by moving daily in the direction of our Vision. What I offer as a coach and speaker is built around my UN philosophy.

—God Bless
Daniel

"For the living know that they will die,
but the dead know nothing, and they have
no more reward, for the memory of them is forgotten"
(Ecclesiastes 9:5, ESV).

"But I don't believe in God!"
"That's alright, He believes in you."

Why

"And let us run with endurance the race
God has set before us"
(Hebrews 12:1b)

WHY *RACING DEATH*?

The reason behind this book is service. Service is the highest pursuit we can take on, and our highest calling. Death is an ominous topic; it scares people, so let's lighten up and focus on living instead. Outside forces are not our greatest issue. The greatest challenges we face come from within. Life can be confusing, and we can struggle to find our purpose, which is the Vision that will sustain us and make us hit the ground running every day. Societal conditioning can make our whole "why" unclear and murky. There is nothing worse than murky.

Choice is a freedom we hold dearly. The freedom of choice is often murkier than we like to think. We can become so conditioned, we fail to choose consciously.

"Better is a handful of quietness than two handfuls of toil and a striving after the wind" (Ecclesiastes 4:6, ESV). This scripture perfectly illustrates how we become conditioned by society and the inherent view of the day. We toil after the shiny stuff of materialistic dreams that we believe will make us happy and content, only to find that there's more to toil for. We're continually chasing things outside of ourselves to make us happy, only to discover that we aren't happy. We need more. Life becomes a

wheel of continual searching for that item, that formula in a book, that holiday, or that affair that will make us feel good once and for all. It usually doesn't happen that way ... luckily. Life's too short to search for that thing we think gives us what we need but will only bring more pain—something we think we need or have been conditioned to believe we need.

It all starts with why! If you can define why you're doing something, or what you want to stop doing, then you'll find success. Think about psychotherapy. What are we really trying to do when we go for this type of help? I want to make it clear that I believe in and encourage this therapy, having used it several times in my life. We're looking to change something in our lives, to understand why that something has power over us, and to change that something so we're no longer under its spell. We need to discover why we are caught up in the habit or pattern.

This book was written to edify you, so might as well go big! I've taken the wisdom I've gained from years of training, racing, coaching, and exploring the ability of humans to challenge personal limits to put into words things that have worked for me and for others. I am an UNlife coach and help people move their personal needles in the directions they want to be moving. I've undertaken this book because understanding your "why" is important. If you can find your "why" through this book, then I've been successful.

My life has been filled with many experiences that have allowed me to explore the deepest, darkest recesses of my mind ... and other weird little places inside of me. I've come through many low moments and experiences. By doing a lot of inner work, I've been able to overcome those experiences that weren't good—experiences that should not have happened, but they did. I made a choice to use the lessons I learned to try and help others find their way through difficulties.

I've had many wonderful experiences as well, and I've explored the brightest, happiest recesses of my mind ... and other weird places inside of me. I discovered that there was a lot of light inside of me, and that I could help shine a light on life for other people. My greatest joy in life comes from helping others achieve their goals or push through their self-imposed limitations. I've been fortunate enough to work my way into places that allow me to fulfill this passion, and I'm grateful for the opportunities life presents for me to do so.

"Why" doesn't have to be intimidating or complicated. Your "why" is what matters when you embrace your life of pursuit. Too often people live the "why" of others who have good intentions but project what they want onto someone else. We're here to take back our "why" and regain personal control. Give yourself the chance to reconnect with your true nature and move toward the thing you know will give your life meaning. Meaning is the great key to happiness, joy, and love.

"Why" is an opening in the energy of the universe for you to walk through and be you. Not someone else's you—life is too short for that. You are a creation of intention by God, and God doesn't make no junk! I hope you have a good time reading this book and that it makes you crinkle your forehead often. Maybe you have lots of questions, and that's really cool. Let's get into this race and have some fun.

"Live Remarkable and Follow the Spirit in Your Heart."
—Daniel K O'Neill

THE UN MANIFESTO

From this day forward, we shall make no excuses. We understand that the power lies within us, and we take that power seriously. Our life is not dictated by the status quo or the limiting mentality that aligns with it. We choose a course of action and boldly pursue our Vision.

Our life is not something that we leave to uncontrolled chance. We are willing to take a chance when pursuing our Vision: it is calculated chance. We are not afraid of risk: we take control of that risk so that others are not pulling the strings in life for us.

VISION

Vision is the template, the blueprint, we have designed for our life. Vision gives us a clear path to follow that will light our way. Our Vision is as unique and special as each of us. We don't allow others to alter, dictate, or criticize our Vision. This Vision of ours is an obsession.

With this very breath, you have the option to step up in pursuit of your Vision. Today, we make our decision to accept the abundance in which we were designed to live, and we will stand in our true nature. We walk in steadfast belief that we were designed for our Vision. When we feel low or down, our Vision will bolster our spirits and carry the day. This is our life right here and right now.

PASSION

We are not passive people ... we are passionate people. We make no apologies for our passion as we pursue it. Our passion and commitment are to strip away the conditioning that keeps us from being true to our Vision. We are not resolved to a life of mediocrity, but to the pursuit of our true nature—bold, willing, and able. We are willing to be indomitable in our pursuit of fulfilling our Vision.

PURSUIT

This life we have is our greatest gift, and we have every intention of UNwrapping it every day. We shall release the entire value of our spirit into the world and share our talents to lift others up. The world is waiting for your energy and spirit.

We are bold enough to understand that today we can create radical change. To be radical means simply going to the root, or to the origin. For each of us, that means living our true nature that was coded on our hearts at birth. We're going to our origin to create a lifestyle we design, control, and implement for that radical change. We no longer live with false perceptions and narratives about who we are and what we are capable of. We radically pursue our Vision with bountiful energy and truth. Today we begin the process to create radical change. Today we become our authentic selves.

We refuse to sacrifice the things that matter most in our lives for those things that matter least. We control and write the narrative of our lives and continually build our pursuit based on that narrative. It is our daily pursuit of our Vision that drives that narrative and builds on it day in and day out. How we act, how we speak, the way we respond, and our daily habits and patterns are all based on a narrative designed to pursue our Vision, which is based on our true nature. We refuse to allow others and society to write our narrative or dictate our Vision and remove our truth. Our intention is strong. Our energy will not waver.

OBSTACLES

We understand that as we pursue life, we will encounter obstacles. We don't shy away from or wither in the face of these obstacles. Obstacles are a way of life. To us they are simply a challenge that will make us stronger, more resilient—and we will overcome them all. Our minds don't hold on to any form of self-pity or allow apathy to set in when faced with obstacles. We rise to a higher level of thinking to solve any problem, and we enjoy the process required to overcome. We understand that obstacles are a means to improve and grow ourselves.

We pursue the lesson the obstacle is offering us rather than focusing on any inconvenience or discomfort it may cause. It's within us to rise above all of our challenges, because we have created a powerful narrative and mindset of perseverance. UNlife hacks become our way; we don't need to have an easy path to achieve our Vision. We understand that if we want to be tougher, then we need to be tougher. Grit is an attitude we relish, and we work hard to make our way.

We understand our power and respect that power. The power to reframe the way we respond to the world around us is our tool. We strive for peace and harmony, yet we will not allow life to beat us down or dictate our way.

GRIT

Our character and attitude are sprinkled heavily with grit. Working hard to master our craft is first and foremost in our minds. When required, we rise up with a solid work ethic that drives us forward in pursuit. We are willing to suffer and bleed for the life we are promised.

There's no fear in us when we step up to face energy that tries to keep us from pursuing our Vision. If gatekeepers appear on the path, we don't give in to the mentality of "No!" If we need to, we will change the rules to get past the gate. Ours is a mindset of and belief in possibility. We are not only passionate, but obsessive about our pursuit.

DEATH

Death has no power over how we live. We race death with exuberant energy and passion. As we pursue life, we choose to not decay or wait for life to come to us. Rather, we are vibrant and willing to touch every facet that makes life possible. Limits are not a way of thinking or living for an UN master. Imposing a limit is to buy into the status quo, and it takes your energy away. Our energy is so intense and focused, we curve our dimension to overcome any limits with our ability through innovation and grit. Death only marks a physical end. Our pursuit is for a greater reward and promise.

JOY

We are unapologetically weird about the joy of our pursuit. It's never our intention to harm others or to impose our will on anyone. We fully understand our societal responsibilities and respect others and their pursuit; however, we will not allow others to compromise our way as we pursue life. Our will to achieve our objectives is strong, disciplined, and joy-filled.

We build joy—in ourselves and our environment—through the glorious way we pursue life in our Vision. Uplifting others is important as we pursue our Vision. In service to others, we create our greatest masterpiece. It's what we are called to do. We excel in the qualities of empathy and compassion. Our nature is one of community and love for one another. If we help another person succeed, we will be raised up higher in our own pursuit. We strive to inspire and motivate others through our example of pursuit. Our energy can and will make a dent in the universe. Ours is a life filled with hope, and we are a part of that hope.

MASTERY

UN is mastery. Mastery is inner peace gained from the process of creating a lifestyle of deliberate practice in which you're working to achieve your Vision and become the best you are capable of being. Mastery is the ability to contain emotion, harness frustration, and channel it all into our pursuit. With mastery we will find a serene way of being that doesn't feel like we are out of control or lost.

Mastery means balancing the mind, body, and spirit into a cohesive unit that has been molded for our Vision. We strive for mastery, as we cannot control anything other than ourselves. To master ourselves means to take the ultimate responsibility for our actions related to thought and intention. Mastering our minds is the greatest reward we can give ourselves. UN means winning in our minds first, and then translating that victory into actions. Those actions are the process we create to achieve our Vision.

UN is building and respecting the Temple. We have but one body that was created for us, and it's designed to be a healthy, thriving organism with unlimited potential and energy. This is where the gift of the Holy Spirit resides along with His ultimate knowledge and wisdom. Turn to the Spirit for guidance, and you will never be lost.

CODE ALIGNMENT

UN requires taking our true nature, which was coded on our heart long before our birth, and releasing the full energy of our spirit. We are not designed to be at the mercy and control of societal conditioning. We are not designed to be conformists. We are not designed to decay and live in apathy and mediocrity.

We are designed to be new wave warriors, moving the needle of change with the code written on our hearts. We choose to take small, deliberate, daily actions to move the needle along and stay true to what we are and see as our Vision. UN is an obsession of faith and trust in a higher power that designed us for our specific Vision.

UN means aligning our skills and abilities with intentional desire to pursue Vision. When we're living UN, we choose lanes of pursuit rather than the crippling ones offered by societal conditioning. UN keeps us from feeling pressured to be and do things we are not. We are the type of warriors who look to enter through the narrow gate rather than through the way of ruin that is wide and enticing. We have a disciplined mind and body, focused on our true nature and Vision. We seek to eliminate bad code and distraction from our path to maintain our values and integrity.

UN means riding on the edge to avoid the comfort zone mentality. UN warriors are mavericks and choose to build a path that takes them away from the status quo to the wilderness mindset. In our wilderness mindset, we seek to connect with the deep-seated authentic connection we have with our very reason for existing. In the wilderness of our mind resides the true message we can carry to the world through our Vision. UN requires trading the conformist rituals of the status quo for the ridiculous energy of pursuit and racing death. Wilderness thinking is about creating a culture that is specific to your pursuit and will sustain your values throughout your journey.

FLOW

UN is being art ... living art that paints the world with your Vision to fill it with beauty and hope. It's that radical change that we are creating because we have the power of Vision. UN allows us to focus on what we want trending in our lives and not on any mediocre conditions. When what we want trending in our lives is flowing, we are flowing in a river of energy that will create and sustain our Vision.

UN means building good structure into your daily life and signing the document of your life with your unique stamp. We question everything in order to ensure that we are not walking aimlessly in conformity by compromising our true nature. UN is being inspired and motivated to living remarkable as you define it.

OPENING THOUGHTS AND DISCOURSE

If you're reading this, then you're alive. That's half the battle ... way to go! I don't have a secret formula for you to follow. I actually don't have any formula at all that will work specifically for you. We are all individuals and unique in our needs, skills, talents, and what will and will not work for us. I'm just being honest about the direction this book is going to go. It requires work on your part. Some of this may seem radical, and that's alright. I'm asking you to be open- minded and think a little gnarly. There's no secret-magic-bullet formula in here ... just ideas I hope will inspire and motivate you.

This is not a "how to" book. If it were, there would be a magic formula in here, but we've already covered that. There are many useful "how to" books out there to help us with specific things in life, like gardening, star gazing, and making a million dollars, but life is much more deep and intricate than those things that can be explained in a "how to" book. Life is not a "how to" journey— it is a "to do" gig. In essence, this is a "to do" book. Life is a wonderful experience wrapped around some tough stuff, a lot of work, some pain, and not always knowing what to do. It can be a real challenge to get up each day and face life. So why not really make it a challenge? We can safely hide under our rock, or we can stand up on top of it and challenge ourselves to be awesome. The challenge is to define what awesome looks like and means to us. Then go out and be awesome, always, and then be more awesome on top of that!

What gives me the authority to write a book like this? My life—my unique, unhealthy, healthy, unbalanced, balanced, energetic, and freaky mind and a mission from God. I've travelled down some roads in life where I've pushed the limits to explore what "awesome" means to me. I've challenged the status quo and pursued the mind of God in those pursuits. What do I mean by that? Well, God has shown me that He is a willing participant in our pursuits when we enter into relationship with Him. That's why I pursue life with a defined lifestyle (some days are a struggle) and energy for adventure. Life is truly a blessing, and we can either chose to be blessed or to be blah!

My objective is not to define how you should walk your own path or what your life should look like. That's not something I should do, and it would be presumptuous of me. I'm writing about a lot of stuff I've experienced through my pursuit of life and breaking through self-imposed personal limitations. Hopefully there are a few things here that will help you create, move into, attempt, and ultimately vigorously pursue your life. I came to a place in my life where I was shown that I'm in a race. That race was outlined years before I was born, or even my parents and grandparents were born. I write from a place that God takes me in our relationship. What you find in this book are ideas that I have had downloaded from a higher power that has never failed to provide for me, comfort me, and more often than I care to reveal, waited patiently while I tried to use my misguided will power to figure it all out. After I fail, God picks me up, pats me on the behind, and sends me out in pursuit again. I'm always looking for His guidance on this path, and He has shown me what will lead me to finding peace. His son promises us a peace offering, a promise that was secured with Jesus' death on the cross so that we may have life. We have within us the seed of a great pursuit that will show us how to race death and move beyond it to a life of radical pursuit. Trust me—you want to be radical.

Here are two key things to know about this book:

1. Death is real, and we are either racing it or we are living dead. This book is based on the mystery of faith. A death that took place over 2,017 years ago on the cross gave us this opportunity.

2. This is a "to do" book—to radically pursue life in your own way by exploring life through some information I share with you.

The following words in bold you will see regularly throughout this book. They are foundational components that are important to this book. I try to explain as best as I can the meaning of these words in relationship to the purpose of this book. Please feel free to add anything you require to these words so they have meaning to you.

MASTERY

I master the pace, that's why I race.
I master my heart, no other reason to start.
I master my mind; it is why I entered the grind.
Mastery is my pursuit;
it is what brings our lives the greatest fruit.
Daniel O'Neill

There is a silent place to which I travel on an inner journey. It is my happy place. It is secluded, quiet, a place of peace. It hasn't always been like this. Once it was full of turmoil, anger, and great sorrow. The path to this place is a physical one; the discipleship, spiritual. We cannot control all aspects of the physical journey in all of its diversity and challenges, but this quest offers us immense opportunity. That opportunity is to become a Master. It's a beautiful process of pain, suffering, joy, love, failure, and eventually victory all rolled into one lifetime. The path to this mastery is a choice between societal conditioning and a path designed for us to experience through the Spirit. The experience and power of a life lived from the perspective of a Master is truly glorious. This is the sum of life wrapped up in one choice: the path of a Master, or the path of wandering from desire to desire.

Mastery is that silent, inner place where we find peace. Inner peace is the spiritual quenching of all life's unbalanced crap. A very wise master told us that we cannot serve two masters. I am not my master; I am a disciple of the Master who chose death over life so that I may chose life over death. The life and peace this decision has brought to me is the game changer.

Mastery means experiencing every aspect of yourself and your life with higher understanding and empathy. All of it—the good, the bad, and the ugly—can be experienced from a higher and more loving perspective. A Master will question everything they know and experience to free their mind from a false place designed for earthly pursuits, instead opening the portal of the spirit where the true pursuit exists. Mastery takes us from the point of reacting in life to a point of creating our life. Over time we become fully immersed in the daily commerce of following the herd rather than creating the circumstances that will benefit our pursuit. Creative living is the cure to living dead. We are in a race for our lives; we are racing death. You are the key to your life. Everything that happens and is required must go through you. The information in this book is provided so that you may take action in your own life. The first thing we all need to do in our lives is take responsibility for where we are, what we have done, and where we want to go. Being accountable is the first step to mastery.

Mastery is a discipline, the choice that we make to be a disciple and look for the way to gain the knowledge and wisdom to achieve that. Mastery is a path of proficiency, and in order to be proficient, we must discover and decide what is truly important to us. To race death is to pursue a spiritual unfolding as we take steps to move along in our pursuit of mastery. Learning is not the ability to gain more information, but the ability to produce the results we truly want in life as opposed to falling prey to those we don't.

Mastery is never a final destination or a completed pursuit. It's an ongoing process of personal growth in the areas we have identified as being important for us. We daily move toward the person, the life, and the relationship with God we desire.

LIFE

This book is all about the pursuit of life, so let's start with life. I find the idea of the human being supremely intriguing. Our design is beyond comparison and scope. I believe that God created us, and there will always be a great mystery surrounding our origins and how we came to be. I am dumb (by dumb I mean dove in) enough to have taken chances in my pursuit of life, and there are things I can share in this book that you may use to dive into your pursuit. My level of dumb is about not cheating on life with an easy-way-out mentality. My level of dumb is to push my personal limits and see what's on the other side. Life is a gift. I wrote this book to hopefully contribute to the human condition and spirit. If this book motivates or inspires one person, then I've been successful. If a mind is opened to its incredible abilities to pursue a new life path, then I'll be happy.

Life is me, you, and everyone we encounter, living in harmony with the ability to pursue and be true to ourselves and the life we were designed for. We can contribute to society and still pursue our own unique state of being as we journey our path. Life is ours to pursue, and we share this habitat together in our pursuits. Let us live a life designed to co-exist with each other in peace.

VISION

This is where it can get scary and confusing, but it doesn't have to be. It gets scary because our internal wiring gets crossed up by societal conditioning. We lose our connection to our true Vision as we try to assimilate into societal norms; this is where we draw our line in the sand. We reboot ourselves and restore our true nature. That's why we pursue life so hard in search of meaning. It's important to know that it's not out there; it's internal and written on your heart. I've learned that life is better when I pursue meaning, not just happiness. We can use this as motivation and energy to more adamantly be that true Vision in our hearts. Let's have fun acknowledging our own unique Vision. We don't have to give away our Vision's power and purpose just because society can't handle the truth and wants to control us with its Vision. Allow yourself to walk a different path, and your happiness and courage will free others to do the same.

I capitalize Vision in this book because of its significance to our pursuit of life. I use it as a hybrid noun/verb. Like you, your Vision is unique, cool, different, and important. I elevate Vision to capital status, because each human is capable of living their Vision and creating change in themselves and their world. What's your Vision for your life? Maybe to stop listening to all the people who mean well with their advice, tests, examples, as this comes from their vision. Our Vision, the one we personally need to hear and live, is within us. We want to focus on reconnecting with our self. On your path, many things will evoke this true nature (Vision) to rise up and be felt and heard through internal feelings. As we experiment in life and pursuit, we become adept at listening to and feeling our Vision.

I'm going to ask you to get real with yourself. Be honest and get to know yourself outside of all the societal conditioning that has covered over the real you. We all wear masks for many different reasons. I'm going to ask you to be brave and not let those societal masks rob you of your Vision. I'll help you find your passion right now. Go to the nearest mirror and look into it. What you see in that mirror is your passion. Yes, it's true, you are your own passion. It all starts with you, with your unique inner truth that no one else can change, alter, or define for you. Give yourself permission to step into the laboratory of life outside all the safe walls you've created. Be gnarly; be radical.

PURSUIT

Ours is a life of pursuit. Over our lifetime we'll pursue many things. Materialism is a pursuit. Love is a pursuit. Mental, physical, and spiritual health is a pursuit. Peace should be a personal and societal pursuit. These all have one thing in common—you pursuing in your life. We should define them on our own terms. I'm pursuing life on my own terms. I follow laws and rules and contribute in societal ways. I don't have to be mindlessly pulled along and spineless as a human being. I can pursue my true nature as written on my heart as a unique expression in the world. To follow societal laws and rules doesn't mean you can't be a nonconformist. One of my big Vision values is to not conform to societal conditioning and to avoid the ways of this world, but that means I have to have my own rules around what nonconformity looks like. I don't want to harm others in my pursuits on this journey. If being a nonconformist means doing that, then I need to re-evaluate why I'm pursuing that action or energy.

Pursuits are much more engrossing, and our eventual success is much higher, when what we pursue is driven from internal intentions and motivations. We need to guide our nature as it was created by designing our lives and how we pursue them. Our own body and spirit are all we can control. We move, live, and pursue through them. Strip away all the materialism, and what you're left with is you. The perfect you as you were created. Your life is important to the overall plan of the created whole that is God's plan.

Life is a beautiful gift. Pursuit is an open road to explore all that you are and all that you can be. There's nothing out there that wasn't first created inside of you. Turn inwards with your focus and discipline, because that's the cornerstone of pursuit. This doesn't have to be complicated. To pursue is to try and get something or do something over a period of time. In our lives we will travel through many seasons. Our objectives need to be designed so that our ultimate pursuit is reached by blowing up the status quo and living a life filled with peace and joy. (I often substitute the word Quest for Pursuit in this work. Cool word, same meaning here.)

HEART

Define heart. That's a difficult thing to do. I've seen heart in action on hockey rinks, football fields, and many different races I've participated in. I've lived it in my life. Trying to put it into words, though, is a difficult thing. Now we have ourselves a challenge, me thinks! Challenges are a good thing, so challenge accepted.

Heart is a measurable attitude; it is a desire, and it is the embodiment of never quitting or giving up. Heart is love of life and the opportunity to live our true nature. Heart is building a temple where our mind and body honour the Spirit. It's using that temple daily to pursue the Vision we were given to live. Heart is taking the pain and knowing you'll survive, you'll be better, and you'll see it all through to the end. Heart takes courage to stand in your Vision against the status quo and live the value in it. Heart is aligning all of your values in a fashion to live a life that fulfills you and delights in the service of others.

The energy of heart doesn't thrive on recognition—it thrives on inspiration. Heart takes the daily, mundane trials and lifts life over the untruth of what society is selling. Heart takes people and turns them into masters of themselves, and then they set a light on the hill for others. The worst circumstances or environments can be overcome with heart. A heart on fire is truly an amazing experience, whether it's your own or someone's with whom you are in contact. Heart and the attitude to beat the heck out of life is a choice—one we make consciously and that requires action every day. It can be built as an energy over which you have creative license. Heart is designing a lifestyle based on your Vision; it's being an active participant in your life and not just a spectator. Heart picks you up and carries you along, because there's no time for pity. Heart is the great force multiplier that will lift us way up above all of it.

DEATH

Death is real, which is why we need to attack life. Our physical death doesn't have to have power over us or signal finality. Christ attacked that mentality and lifestyle by enduring the cross for us. He who believes never dies—our bodies yes, but our spirit, never. We have a choice here and now as we walk the path every day. Choose the narrow gate and attack life with all of your heart to enter through that gate. There is great energy in pursuing God's wisdom. It doesn't limit us; it unleashes us and frees us. That's how to attack life and release yourself from the daily lifestyle of death. Question everything, even God. If you're questioning God, it means you're having conversations with Him.

There's a release of energy when we pursue life because we want to live authentically by racing death. That makes you a courageous person, a willing participant in racing death to pursue life. If you don't attack life authentically, then you are living dead. Why sell yourself and this gift of life short? That's not how you were designed or what you have to be resigned to. As long as you aren't hurting others in your radical pursuit, then you're doing it right. You're attacking life; racing death means you stand up and make actionable what you see in your Vision. Death is not an option to live; it has already been conquered by the cross ... now we live.

MOVE THE NEEDLE

Progress is the objective. We want to be progressing toward self-mastery and personal peace, but we often measure ourselves against a standard that isn't relative to us. It comes from societal conditioning, and it's unrealistic to measure ourselves against these outside forces. Younger people really struggle with this today. Within the social media world, it appears like everyone is walking down happy-camper street.

You are fine the way you are. We are not broken and in need of fixing. I've had to fight this mentality in my journey. For way too long, I thought there was something wrong with me, that I was broken and needed to be fixed. That was just my self-pity party attitude, and it cost me time and energy. I was measuring myself against the gauge of society and trying to move a needle that didn't belong to me. I was trying to move needles that led me to that idea of being broken and in need of fixing. That's called learning and growing.

Life truly is amazing and worth draining every ounce of energy out of. I had to make a personal shift in my attention from the societal needle to my own personal needle. I had to identify those things that made sense to me and had meaning for me ... things I was willing to sacrifice, work, and suffer for to push the needle in the right direction. We determine the right direction in which to move—not what society says, and not the status quo.

"You were running well. Who hindered you from obeying the truth?" (Galatians 5:7, ESV). To discover your own needle, you need to go inside and do a little self-discovery. Get to the root (Radical Pursuit) of who God made you to be. This is where the needle gets big, beautiful, and really exciting and bold. Boldness is radical, and you, my friends, are capable of being bold beyond your wildest imagination. Go there too ... to your wildest imagination. There is value in being audacious in your needle settings!

It's important to measure your progress as you work toward the outcome you want to create. Take the time to work out the metrics you find acceptable and inspiring to measure the journey. Get on the right frequency for you and move the needle according to your desired way.

SOCIETAL CONDITIONING

Societal conditioning is the biggest killer of pursuit. It's a constant battle to not allow ourselves to live dead because of societal conditioning. The energy required to not fall into this way of thinking and being seems immense and can be draining, because we've wandered away from the true nature we were born with and that sustains us. As our education and indoctrination moves along, we don't even see that we are trading our true, vibrant, and exuberant nature for controlling and limiting societal conditioning. That true nature never leaves you and can be regained. It will open you to a pursuit that will flourish and make life exciting and unique.

I am talking here about radical change and a personal revolution to free you from all the limiting information and controlling mind education we are subjected to. The true light and way is ours to live in continually and in every way, but we must free our minds from the way they are bombarded daily to take us away from the truth. Society requires a level of buy-in from the people who occupy it. There needs to be a form of conformity amongst people so that we co-exist in a safe, healthy, and prosperous way with each other; however, the herd mentality common today goes way beyond the type of simple conformity we need. And let's be honest … is the way we live all that free and prosperous on all levels? We have higher debt, greater health and mental health issues, increased crime … man, this list could go on. Is this really the way you think life should unfold? If this is how you envisioned it, then don't read on … that's cool. If this is nowhere near how you saw it, then maybe you're not connected fully with your true nature.

The radical pursuit we face means returning to the root of who we are. That's simply what radical means … returning to the root of something. We don't give away our control or true nature, but gaining this kind of freedom is truly amazing and moves the needle of our energy, enthusiasm, and kingdom living to new heights on our pursuit path. The truth is written in a book thousands of years old, and that is where our real knowledge and wisdom lies. We can build our lives around this wisdom and knowledge, freeing ourselves from conditioning that limits us and takes captive our truth. Today we make the change to free that truth from conditioning and pursue life.

TRUE NATURE

We were born with a code written on our hearts. That code came from our Creator and will never be removed from the inner place where the Spirit resides. This is the truth we were designed to live and the way we were created to be during our time on earth. A lot of stuff along the way likes to push this code down and try to rewire us. Societal conditioning is the number one offender that attacks and tries to undo this truth so that we come into compliance with the status quo. We have an innate ability to always come back to this true nature—if we decide to live that code.

God is a far better code writer than society. Your true code never goes bad or expires, but it does require updates in order to be truly experienced and expressed in our lifetime. You are the master of the journey when you tap into the code. In relationship with God, we experience the great teacher who wrote the code and will do everything in His immense power to create the way, the light, and the truth for us to experience the proper code. True nature is rewarding and fulfilling, but not always easy to take, and it can be a struggle that will take us to many difficult places and through some unique experiences. That's the true beauty of anything really worthwhile. If it were easy, everybody would be doing it. Seek first that which is in your heart, for the truth contained therein is from the Good News. It's a powerful message that will set you free to embrace the real person you were meant to be.

KINGDOM LIVING

"But seek first the kingdom of God and his righteousness, and all these things will be added to you" (Matthew 6:33, ESV). We already have the kingdom within our midst, although it's tough to see in this day and age with all the turmoil in our world. Hate, violence, and politics are all around us, and there seems to be no end in sight. I wish I had the answer. I do have it at my disposal to use for myself, as does everyone else. It's in the Word, and it's as appropriate today as when it first came onto the scene.

Even if you don't believe in God or Jesus, can living by what the Word offers be bad? Even if the thought of God is beyond you, does the content of the Bible somehow become less important? *"But the fruit of the Spirit is love, peace, patience, kindness, goodness, faithfulness, gentleness, self-control; against such things there is no law"* (Galatians 5:22, ESV). If you're an atheist, I'm not here to convert you. Would you agree, though, that the things listed in this scripture verse are worth pursuing? We can and should live by these basic values and principles. Societal conditioning asks that we be this way yet makes no laws or efforts to keep them as core values. The world is full of wolves who will take advantage of a lack of core values within society. (That's why we require sheepdogs.) Kingdom living is seeing these things as the path to peace and loving thy neighbour as thyself. I don't care in what book that comes from—it's worth living.

The kingdom given to us is found in the many promises offered to us in the Bible. Yes, we are asked to do some work—that's something we need to understand. Your desire to pursue the kingdom is up to you. Seeing through the glitter and glory of the day to the way of the kingdom is difficult. My one piece of advice for you is this:

> *Enter by the narrow gate. For the gate is wide and the way is easy that leads to destruction, and those who enter by it are many. For the gate is narrow and the way is hard that leads to life, and those who find it are few.* (Matthew 7:13, ESV)

We have the opportunity to focus on the wisdom and knowledge found in our relationship with God and in scripture. It's not an easy path; it takes work, dedication, and discipline. Societal conditioning offers us the wide-open spaces of conforming to the ways of this world. It looks shiny and pretty but leads to destruction. Our gate is waiting for us to enter. Today is that day, my friend; your actions will determine which path you walk. The reward is beyond anything my words can describe.

MY FAITH

I am a Christian, and this book is built on Christian principles. I use some scripture to illustrate the unique opportunity we have to live a life with the creator of all we see. To walk with God and enjoy an intense, loving, nourishing, and mind-opening relationship with Him is at the heart of all this writing. I'm not an expert in the Bible or all things Christian. As a matter of fact, I live on the edges of the Christian mindset and model. I'm not into religion or dogma; I'm into God and pursuing the life He has shown me.

You may not like some of what I write. I'm cool with that and understand if you don't. Your prerogative is up to you, and my theme in this book concerns living your true nature and following what's right for you. My goal in this book is to harm no other person. If what I write or put forth offends you, then that's your choice. This is an open view of my mind going medieval. Going medieval is about taking control of your mind and body and allowing God to be the driving force in that process through your spirit. I'm sharing with you what has driven me to overcome the societal conditioning that limits us in our pursuit of life.

We've all built some false limitations into our minds over time. If I could encourage you to do one thing with this moment you have right now it would be to tear down those limitations and expose them for the frauds they are. Don't allow societal conditioning or voices from your past to design any form of limiting belief or thought.

Your potential and the potential of the energy that created you are much greater than any limit your mind could entertain. Always be safe and aware that you're human and don't put yourself in danger; however, the danger of your self-imposed personal limitations is not acceptable. The world isn't static; it's continually changing and moving, because it is energy. Nothing you are right now is fixed and has to be a permanent state.

Find your extreme, radically pursue your life, smile and wave a lot, and joy will follow you all the days of your life.

RADICAL ENTRY 1:

Radical Pursuit

*"So then let us pursue what makes for peace
and for mutual upbuilding"*
(Romans 14:19, ESV).

A WANDERING SPIRIT

I have a restless, wandering spirit. When I was a younger, it was a source of pain and suffering for me, because I didn't understand its beauty and the source of power it would be for me. Because it was something I didn't understand or pursue, I made some really bad choices for my spirit—things I didn't understand at the time, because I didn't listen to my spirit. Instead, I was swayed by the grandeur of the marketing and societal lies around me. The system is set up to produce good, willing, and productive inhabitants. Of course, that is all defined by the production-line-refinery mentality that brought forth the amazing fortunes and lifestyles we see in society today.

Progress was good for many, but for others it was a bundle of sticks that would be their burden to carry for generations, especially if they were controlled by a mindset that said "this is what's best for all," or "this is what will liberate and free you all." This form of peace was sold to the masses as the world began to change during the industrial revolution, and it's still pursued today. It's easy to believe and follow, because we've been programed to follow this path—a simple, single code designed to keep the status quo (peace as prescribed for the status quo).

As a young man, I couldn't wrap my mind around this form of peace; for me, it wasn't real. Sure, I could play along and do my part. I understand that need and am grateful for the level of health, wealth, and general societal normalcy that I have experienced. It would be a lie to say I accepted that as the truth and as my true purpose. Real peace for me was a mystical, far away fantasy. I couldn't fathom having peace of any kind—mental, physical, or even spiritual. As a matter of fact, I actually liked the pain and inner turmoil I was experiencing, and it became my security blanket. My mental state was dark and foreboding, and it washed over and subdued the inner qualities of a restless spirit wanting to explore and create adventure. Time would show me that what I was actually experiencing was the disruptive force that was my spirit. This inner spirit was saying "No way, dude, not in your lifetime." A battle raged inside of me between the guiding, living spirit and my noggin. My mind was wrapped up in the world outside of spirit, buying the societal mythology that would have me be a good conformist and contributor. Real peace escaped me ... at times, painfully.

I'm now fifty-four years old, and a lot of water has gone under the bridge. The beautiful thing about water is it keeps flowing. Man, I love being close to flowing water. Streams, rivers, creeks, and brooks are places of learning, growing, and healing for me. My spirit brings me to these places for growth and expansion, or to just get over myself. They say you can never put your foot into the same river twice, because as it flows the water is always different. I've come to know and believe that our personal bodies and lives are the same. At no time are we exactly the same person we were yesterday. We continually change, grow, and evolve in all areas. We have a choice in this whole process, too. We can choose to be alive and part of the pursuit. We are either aware and cognizant of this fact and living to pursue this path, or dead and letting the world around us dictate who we are. Setting that wandering, curious, loving, and powerful spirit within us free is really a good thing ... trust me.

I'M A RADICAL

To be radical is simply to return to the root of the thing. I define a radical pursuit as the art of recapturing our true nature before it was stripped away by societal conditioning. The true beauty of ourselves is there waiting to be restored so we can live authentic lives. Being radical is not a bad thing in terms of the etymology of the word. It simply means going to the origin. Well, we are created in the image of God, which is our essential nature, so let's get back there. I'm radical in my pursuit of this powerful pathway, and you can be as well. The path I pursue fills me with energy; my heart is now filled with light, as yours can be too. I'm radical in the sense that I see the world in a different dimension than I used to. Life has a quality and substance to it that elevates my restless spirit to the place it feels and lives in harmony with the world. You can experience this in your inner self and outer walk. It feels wonderful to be on this path.

This path takes work; it isn't an easy path to follow. It's a daily struggle to stay on the way and not stray. We often fail to uphold the way and have to fight our old patterns and habits as they try to work their way back into our lives. I've discovered on the journey to this point in my life that I'm a bit of a loner. My nature requires a lot of soulful, quiet, and off-by-myself introspection time. I lean toward places where there are small crowds or none at all. Part of the path I follow requires congregating with other people of like mind and faith. Part of my calling on this path is to uplift others and carry their heart and minds in a compassionate and loving way. Inspiring and motivating others makes my spirit soar. I find no greater passion or joy than seeing others achieve their goals and pursue their lives full on. Being part of that pursuit honours my energy, and I'm brought to higher levels of joy.

The great thing about this path and the radical pursuit of it is how it impacts every area and facet of our lives. From the smallest of things to the biggest in life, what we pursue and want to experience on the path will create an immense peace in, around, and through us. Life is worth living, which is why we want to radically pursue it—to experience life to the fullest and actually be ALIVE as we pursue it. I guess it can sound a little weird when I put it that way, but I know what it's like to live DEAD—dead in the sense of being devoid of spirit, purpose, and adventure, and not even want to go on with life. It takes way more energy to face and live life dead. I've become adept at reading myself and my moods. I can have dark and brooding spells as I journey. I know that these are brought on by not focusing on what I can control. Instead, I focus on the things over which I have no control, and that energy begins to consume me. I now know that these moods mean I need to stop being self-centred and turn my attention to the one who brought me to my path—Christ!

I choose LIFE over DEATH, and Christ has shown me that there is a truth to the restless quality of my spirit, which is that I don't want to just settle. I don't find any peace in materialism and its pursuit. I've tried that path, and it's a path that leaves one empty. There's always another desire … not a need, but a desire. The shine eventually wears off and more is required—bigger, better, and more expensive.

During that stage, I chose not to believe in God. I tried to make myself the master of my path. I tried the willpower trap, and it just led to frustration. Willpower didn't help me understand the restless nature of my spirit; instead, I tried to will myself into a way of being that wasn't true to my nature. I created a pattern of living that caused me to live dead! As I walked this path, I encountered many people who were also dead like me. I've grown to see that there is an alternative to living dead, which I now radically pursue. I pursue life; it is life filled with wonder and joy, and it's fulfilling. I admit there is a component of mystery to this radical pursuit; it's part of the path.

RACING DEATH

It's radical to choose death in pursuit of life, yet that death will provide us with life. Are you confused yet? It's all part of the mystery. People have tried to prove and disprove this mystery for a long time. It's one of those mysteries in life that each person needs to explore in their own way. The mystery is rewarding and will provide you with great direction in your life on your radical journey. Mysteries invite us to solve them; they invite us to figure them out. This mystery of faith, however, is one to be lived. To believe it and walk it out is to receive the reward and abundant benefits of the death that began the mystery. The part that will be solved comes after that earthly death we will all encounter. I choose to be radical in how I pursue the mystery, and it has been more than worthwhile.

The appetite for the path, along with our own nature to pursue this mystery, makes it a radical pursuit. We can all partake in this radical way of living, being, and chasing the death we deserve. God comes into our lives in unique and cool ways. As we journey, we'll discover activities, places, and messages that are unique to the nature God called us to. God wants us to live with extreme energy and pronounced gusto. He has always known what we need, how our needs are tied in with our nature, and how we can best tap into our strengths. We are more of a mystery to ourselves than to God. The mystery of faith in death creates our pursuit of life. It's a radical pursuit because we are connecting through faith with the energy of God.

What is it that creates the faith required for me and you to pursue this path, this relationship? Love from God and of God drives this radical pursuit of life through faith. This love is validated through faith, not by the scientific standards of today. This faith comes from what I have seen and experienced in my life (and continue to experience). A big part of this faith is to question it, put it to the test! I don't blindly follow a doctrine or a law for the sake of being right, or for the belief that I'm better than those who don't. Conversely, I put this faith to the test. I question it, ponder it, and full on explore it. I create my own scientific experiments to pursue this faith relationship with God.

Through my experiments in faith, I've discovered that God pursues us much harder than we can pursue Him. I've experienced the grace, love, guidance, abundance, peace, and joy of God in all areas of my life. God has touched and created in my life in ways that I never could have created on my own. My life has become much more stable, rewarding, fulfilling, and filled with goodness since my energy has been directed into my radical pursuit.

This is not an easy path to pursue. It's even harder to be radical about it. The Christian life is difficult, and it can sometimes seem impossible. Our society, dictated in many ways by a non-Christian attitude toward life, tempts us to be anything but Christian. I struggle daily with the path I have chosen to pursue, and some days I totally fail to achieve my goals. I need to have deep faith in God's truth and His absolute love for me. It's an exciting feeling to experience the power of the Holy Spirit moving through me and providing for me; understanding how God is actually moving through the Spirit in my physical space and time still blows my mind. Feeling the Spirit create energy in me that then moves out into fields of action in my daily radical pursuit is phenomenal.

THE BIG QUESTION

If there is one great lesson in life, I believe this is it: every day we have a choice. It's actually simple and doesn't take a whole lot of energy, yet it can become the all-consuming focus of our lives. Daily we chose to pursue life or death. Ponder it for a moment. It could be the biggest question you will ask yourself today. When I step out of this bed today, will I pursue what I really want to be? Will my actions align with my values and morals? At the end of the day when I climb back into this bed, will I have chosen a day lived over a day spent dead?

I encounter people every day whose sole purpose is to just get through the day. A lot of these people are making a bunch of money with all the material trappings. They have everything money can buy—great jobs and families, and powerful positions (as they define power). Yet their days are drudgery and pain-filled because they aren't happy. They're spending and searching outside of themselves, and their credentials have not met their expectations or filled their inner void. Credentials are awesome, aren't they? We hang them on walls to remind us of who we are, trapped in a place that may not be true to our nature, but man … look at this office and position! Don't let your credentials cloud who or what you may really be.

For these people, their search for meaning has been circumvented by a level of thinking that is designed to actually keep them from living. Death has already caught them in a vice and is driving the train—so much to buy, grab, and identify with on the material side of the life ledger. Their jobs define their worth, and their quality of life is determined not by joy, happiness, and relationship, but by needs and desires. Why are there so many unhappy people in the world? Because they have chosen death- filled living and consumerism over a life filled with the pursuit of their potential and adventure.

My radical pursuit of life isn't selfish or based on any material object. I race death every day of my existence, and my pursuit is filled with hope, joy, light, and life. I see myself in a position at the end of my life where I have served people and my Creator well. I see myself having lived a life where death is not a sad thing for my loved ones and my friends. My outward expression of peace and joy will be my legacy, and I will go to rest knowing what awaits me.

We have an example that can help us along the path as we journey. Jesus is our strength, Lord, and earthly example. I don't blindly follow a doctrine or give up myself as a denial of my human nature. I continue to tell people that I am a sinner; it is my aim, my goal and my radical pursuit to reduce the sins in my life as much as possible. If I can significantly reduce the negative impact my actions and choices have on those around me and the world, then I am pursuing well. I challenge myself to take care of and treat my body well, which is home to the Holy Spirit. This gift of life is bestowed on believers in Christ through His death. Beautiful and off the beaten path, I pursue that death of love so I can hopefully express it in all I do. It's a radical process in the truth, and the truth today is not a sought-after commodity. I can live deficient of any negativity and emotional pain or suffering because I'm connected to pure love, and you can be too if you choose it.

Each second of every day we have the opportunity to pursue an amazing moment of living in pursuit of God. I can't focus on death as an imminent event, robbing myself of right now. It's full steam ahead, man. I'm racing death in every way possible so that when the time comes, it will be a welcome visitor in a life well lived. I don't have time to worry about death, because God has told me to push it out of the way.

DEATH IS NOT THE ENEMY … LIFE IS!

We choose to spend our lives trying to fill a void, but there is no void to fill. We simply have to live. On the surface we see ourselves living, barely sometimes. In a life of pursuit, there's no void, no "barely" living. There's a heartfelt Vision with which we are in touch and can feel deep inside that drives us along and gives us energy. Our sense of purpose doesn't come from what others think about us or what we want others to think about us. It comes from a desire to pursue the gift of helping others be the best they can be. To serve is to live, and that living brings the pursuit to a beautiful place in our daily lives.

Death has no grip on a human that pursues and walks with the death of the cross. It's only a shadow that follows us, hoping to bring us down. There's no power in earthly death; it means nothing. I don't look forward to it, for sure ... that's natural. Yet I don't live a life filled with fear that keeps me from truly living and pursuing the wonders of the world. Radically accept death and then race it and choose to fill time with living rather than worrying.

Live healthy, eat healthy, and practice things that will add years to your life. That's called sensible living and honouring the temple that is your body. Take time to exercise and push the mental and physical limitations we put on ourselves because of what society has taught us. Be honest in your assessments of where you are and how you are living. Be kind and gentle when you stumble but set an indomitable focus and discipline in your convictions to live. Death doesn't dictate life; in the end, it is the definition of life and how we lived.

Erase death from your timeline. When you look ahead into the future, don't look at age and time as finite. We have no idea how long we can or will live. To focus on the end of the timeline is to give away the power of now—right now, right here. This moment is your opportunity to pursue life instead of death. Make choices based on that Vision inside and step into the energy that is available to realize that Vision. Let go of some old beliefs, question everything, and be open to things you felt were not possible.

Death has no power in a heart that embraces the truth of faith and the unknown beyond the physical end of this body. When we're done with this body and our energy centre, the spirit returns to its source. What then? Life beyond comprehension! Ascending to our place beside our creator to talk, laugh, and receive the reward! Life moves us to death's door ... that's non-negotiable and inevitable, but the terms on which we live are negotiable. Sink all you have into this pursuit, and you'll be beyond amazed at what results await you. Crazy, radical pursuit of life will bring you into a place of self-awareness that will make death fade from your fearing mind and push you into a race that's worth running.

CHANGE THE SHAPE

We are not broken, we are not lost ... we are just out of shape. For many years I really thought that I was broken. Abuse messes up your mind. It takes a piece of you; actually, it rips out a piece of you. I'm not sure I'll ever get that piece of me back. I've struggled with a lot of anger issues that have hampered me, hurt relationships, and kept me out of shape. My driving force is the desire to change the shape of that pain, that energy, and those thoughts. Blowing up the status quo has been a big part of the equation in that force. I've never used that abuse as my platform. It happened, and I can't change that. Re-organizing my thoughts and mind around it is changing the shape of me. That's what I can control and take action on. Rehashing all that took place won't change the shape of me, so my platform is to help people realize that they don't have to stay stuck and out of shape.

The shape to share some of my trials is required in my platform to show others a way out of their shape. We need to be more active in victims' rights and stopping abuse. We need to believe people when they come forward and not make them feel as if they were at fault. We need to create safe and secure options for abuse victims, sexual assault victims, and people who are bullied. If that has to be my platform, then my story is worth sharing.

The shapes you have in your life are a choice. It's been a real tough journey for me along this path. The amount of "woe is me" energy I've expended on the slights of my life is massive. I shaped myself as a victim, and that shape played a role in much of my life. Being the victim was easy, and it gave me an out. I based and built my shape around the emotion of the past, effectively giving away my personal power. I allowed life circumstances, life events, life rules, people, and whatever else to dictate to me. I was not lost ... I was accepting a choice to stay in the shape of helplessness. Maybe that is harsh, but I don't think so. I was living dead; it was a choice, and I lost a lot of life and joy because of it. I chose to allow the shape of anger to dictate my life in all areas, fostering the shape of self-pity, and feeling sorry for myself when things didn't go my way. It took a choice to get the shape of my mind right, and then it took a lot of grit and determination to turn that shape into a new way of being.

The power to take personal responsibility for all the shapes in our lives is inside of us. Stepping up into the shape of being self-aware and self-directed while taking responsibility for all we are is important. We have a chance to be an active participant in our own shape-shifting as we decide to take on this personal responsibility. This understanding and change in attitude was changing the shape of my mental energy, and it spread. I started to choose to be more active in my fitness objectives. I chose to be more active in social interactions and social events. Life started to change shape around me, which was brought on by the shifting of perceptions because of my choices. I faced many struggles, because so many of my habits and patterns had become entrenched in my living. It took time to move the needle, but daily actions made small changes in me.

It was at this time and juncture in my life that I started to get truly radical, returning to the root of my life. We need to look at the root causes of why we end up taking the shapes we do and being in the shape we're in. Getting into shape required a trainer, a coach to help me learn and grow and who would push me into the areas that would require me to change. Interestingly, my trainer chose me, not the other way around. God was willing to show me the light, and He showed me the true way to change my shape in a lasting and truly awesome way. God promises us in Romans 12:2 that He will transform our minds. That was the root cause of my bad shape— a mind that was a little bent.

My mind wasn't broken, but it was bent. The shape it had taken on wasn't aligned with my true nature. I had a coach who was showing my daily and in His radical ways that I could reshape that mind into an image He had intended for it from my birth. Hope is an amazing gift in life. It's a means to creating and maintaining a better shape. Change the shape of your life with the wisdom and knowledge of a great trainer who will make the shape you achieve the best you've ever had.

RECESS

Recess was my best subject when I went to school ... well, that and Physical Education. I don't think you can say Physical Education any longer, but because this is my book and I'm older, too bad! Since I excelled at recess, I have actively, voraciously, and excitedly pursued recess-like experiments and events in my life. That's a great way to make an example of how we can use what works for us to pursue life. It took me a long time to learn that work is what we do so we can enjoy the things in life that really matter. I like doing things that really matter. To define myself though my writing, the charitable work, and the fitness is so much more important than defining myself through my work life. I take my recess seriously, folks.

Doing an Ironman or other endurance events is what I would consider a recess. These are the things I do to make my life exciting and fun. This type of pursuit moves my needle and my spirit energy in the direction I need it to go. Fun is important to me. There are times I've taken certain things too seriously, and they were things that really were low on my totem pole of meaning. Learning is something I've talked about as an important part of our pursuit. There were some tough lessons along the way for me about where I was directing energy that would never offer a full return. That's something I had to really challenge myself in to move the energy to a different focus with more return. That shift is an important moment in our lives. It's the moment when we realize that we aren't focusing our energy where we need it to be. This shift is an opportunity to shift our energy and perspective. If we make the decision at this time, we can create the new energy we want and direct it toward that thing we know will make a difference.

I remember sitting and looking at the clock, waiting for recess. I get the same feeling before my adventures in training and racing. Some adventures involve trips my wife and I take to do races. Those are cool recesses from the world of work and other obligations. It's not a form of escape that has no purpose other than trying to get away from what you don't like. I've met many people who set up elaborate vacations and enjoy them, yet they come back and the dread of work and life take over again. Any benefits from the vacation are gone quickly. Recess isn't about escaping; nope, it's about exploring—exploring the world in a way that allows you to express control and your true nature.

Recess is an unlimited event that crosses all our boundaries of societal conditioning. We can condition our own needs and ways to access energy for our pursuit, and recess is a tool we can use to create that childlike awe and excitement life often removes as we get older. We need to learn to make that freedom a part of all aspects of our lives. To not have the freedom to pursue what makes us feel alive is living dead. Take a recess break every day and do something off the chain that makes you feel good. Get off the couch and walk through a field with your imagination and nothing else keeping you from being the Vision you are in pursuit of.

Suppressed Spirit

If there's one thing I've learned and continue to struggle with it's this: supressing my spirit by trying to be something or someone I'm not will focus energy in places that will create negative consequences. Rather than allowing my spirit to flow and flourish in my world, I sometimes gravitate toward a conforming spirit.

We all need to interact at times on levels or in situations that aren't ideal. Sometimes we have to experience discomfort and unhappiness, because that's a part of life. No one said life was fair. How we respond to these situations and the impact they have on us is important. I've learned through my spirit that we have the ability to respond in life; we don't have to react. Reacting often comes from an emotional place and takes us down a road we will regret. Responding is the ability to choose how and if you will respond in any way at all. You don't have to accept invitations to things in life you don't want. You can simply respond by walking away. "Peace out" to whatever is trying to provoke or limit you.

If we allow it, society can beat us down. That's not life—that's society piling its conditioning on top of you. Life is different; life is a gift that was offered to you when you were conceived. You have a choice when you wake up every day. You can choose life, or the surface-existence society offers. You're much deeper than that surface, and your spirit will rock the world if you allow it to be free. In our politically correct and scared-to-offend society, we give up our spirit power easily and, most often, unknowingly. We don't want to offend; we don't want to be singled out. Early in our lives we're conditioned to try and fit in and not question the hierarchy and system. We pull our spirit into our shell and keep it quiet so we don't create any waves.

Other people don't have to believe in God, as that's a free choice He gives to us all. Other people may not understand this spirit connection, but that shouldn't dictate how you connect with your spirit. Hey, other people may even question your sanity. That's good; it's always a little cool to have people wonder what you're really all about. It keeps them off balance, and you shouldn't be concerned with their opinion of you. You can always use that perception to your advantage. Pursue life in the manner you need that allows you to express your spirit energy in all that you do. Be aware and alive in your knowledge that the Spirit resides within you, and that power is your pursuit launch point.

BALANCE

There will be things we like in our lives and things we don't like. We have good days and we have bad days. There are things we want to do and things we have to do. Life is a constant strain between the yin and yang of balance. Finding and maintaining balance in life can be difficult. We have a finite amount of time in each day, and our time is often consumed by more "have to dos" than "want to dos." That's life; often it feels that this is the norm. It can be draining and frustrating.

Our lives can be overrun by this lack of balance. Like a garden where weeds choke out the good growth, our desired lifestyle can be choked out by all of those "have to dos" and societal conditioning. Over time we succumb to those norms and become numb to our true nature. Slowly we die, our inner garden gets overrun, and our dreams no longer stoke the fire in our heart. Balance is lost, and there is no equality in our entire lifestyle.

We sacrifice time for our wants because, well, we don't want to be perceived as selfish. Saying no to things that erode your "want to dos" isn't being rude, nor does it make you a bad person. When you protect your Vision and take the time to create a balanced life that allows you to pursue life on your terms, you're actually looking after your health. Balance is not an act but a measure that we should design into our lifestyle. When we create balance that allows our energy to be directed into our Vision, we can be more complete in all areas of our lives. If you want to improve your relationships, work, health, and success in following your Vision, creating balance is key.

Say no! We have the right to say no to busyness and unhealthy demands on our time. We have to learn to protect our time. How often do we find ourselves bogged down in time-eating stuff that just has no value? I'll talk later about distraction and the impact it can have on our lives. We need to find our balance. Let me say that again a little louder: "We need to find OUR balance."

Balance provides a sense of control and normalcy. We need to move to a balanced place where what is most important for us is front-of-mind focused. Being realistic is important, as is dividing out time between our own needs and those of others. Being caught in a vortex of other people's needs and time is not acceptable. At the top of your mind should be your Vision. Be respectfully selfish with your energy and time so that you're on balance in your mind, body, and spirit. That way you are far more effective for others.

FREEDOM

Yup, freedom; apparently, we have it. Supposedly we live it and we claim to be thankful for it. I can't understand why so many people are unhappy in our society. If freedom is the most important aspect of being a human, then in our society people should be beyond ecstatic and happy.

We have the illusion of freedom wrapped in the societal way of controlling that freedom. If you pursue life in manner A, we, the people, accept you. If you pursue life in manner B, we, the people, may alienate, ostracize, and consider you a freak. You may be labelled as a rebel or a radical, and your mental faculties may be questioned. Society doesn't like change or change agents unless it stands to gain from it, so we're told to follow a brand of freedom and we'll fit in and have a good life.

Freedom starts with the ability to pursue life on our own terms, in our own truth, with our own thoughts, and with no intention to harm others. We are born complete, but we are trained and conditioned in systems designed to maintain order and control. These systems are not always based on what is best for us or our definition of freedom.

Live inside yourself in a free way—free to express your unique nature and live it out in your daily walk. Take off the veil of societal conditioning if it's keeping you from being who you really want to be. Freedom is the choice to conform and contribute as a member of society in the way we choose. We all have a responsibility to contribute, but we are free to choose how we contribute. Freedom consists of choice designed by true nature and lived in our own way.

Life is an opportunity to promote true freedom. Each man, woman, and child is a free will ambassador. Our world is now open to so many paths to express true freedom. A life of pursuit involves moving energy daily into freedom of spirit.

VALUE

I value a lot of personal privileges, such as personal space and time and the ability to work and make a living. I value my health and wellbeing. Democracy is important to me and of great value in our society. A sense of purpose and personal connection with life is of value to me. I value human rights and the rights of others, so I place value on daily aspects of life and how they impact my ability to pursue my Vision. The spirit within us is of immense value for our journey and expressing our true nature. It's valuable to our sense of wellbeing and our means to interact, express love, and pursue life. This value is steady and true. We can bank on it being our guiding value with great energy infused into it.

The Spirit will never guide us in a harmful or wayward manner. Pure Vision and goodness are ours to access and use daily. They're built right into and written on our hearts the moment we are conceived. God gives us free will in how we use, approach, and live our lives. His good code is written there for us to value and use. Life can really cross up our value and values. We value so much outside ourselves that we suppress the true value stored up for us. The mind becomes the focal driving point of all our daily transactions. We believe that we can control our goals, dreams, aspirations, and success with our mind, and it creates false value.

Success in anything comes from the heart, where God stored up all wisdom, energy, knowledge, and success when He wrote your code. We suppress this code when we cross this value. We're human and it happens. Remember this—the code written on your heart never disappears or goes bad. When you throw yourself headlong into pursuit of life, it will explode out of you and create energy and momentum.

Creating true value as you define it is important for your pursuit and how you see yourself as an individual. Your true value will change anything in your life if you allow yourself to truly express and experience it. Defining that value can be a little difficult, but it isn't impossible, even in a consumer-driven economy with all the negative stuff we're faced with daily. Search inside yourself and listen to the still, quiet inner guide that will show you the way. The Spirit understands what you need and will guide you to true paths to find that unique value you are designed to share with all of us, and we are waiting.

CREATIVITY

I used to consider myself one of the least creative people alive. I never looked at myself as creative or even having any creative ideas. I judged myself against the high profile artistic stuff in the world around me. It's easy to look at the mainstream of art and creativity and feel that you may not measure up. We love to compare in our society, and keeping score is a big thing in societal conditioning, but it can create internal perspectives that aren't true. Someone is always better at that one thing, so we have a choice to make; we are at a crossroads. We can focus on the belief that we'll never be that good, skilled, talented, or creative, or we can refuse to focus on anything else but ourselves and getting better at our craft.

God did something that really helped me see that this personal perception wasn't accurate. He told me to lighten up … pretty much in those words too. I needed to consider things at a deeper level. I needed to mine the truth and really give myself an opportunity to experience my creativity. If you're going to argue with God, you'd better come up with something besides, "Well, what do you know!" He proceeded to ask me to write a book. When I learned not to supress my creativity by thinking in terms of getting it all right, my world changed. I just figured out that if I shipped it without the idea of perfection, I was at least shipping. Time allows us to rework the past, and then we can remake what we felt wasn't our best work. Writing my first book was a challenge because I wanted it to be just so, to be close to perfection. Then one day my publishing assistant told me to just write it. I released my conditioning that a book had to be perfect before being published. Had this not happened, that first book never would have been released and its value never known.

In order to be creative, we need to understand how we can release our creative potential. Be creative with the energy of the Spirit which flows with power and authority inside of you. It's all about releasing over suppressing. When we open ourselves to the Spirit, download the truth, and capture our true nature, we can run with our creative side and crank up the pursuit of life. Believe in yourself and your talent and give yourself permission to pursue creativity. The creativity I'm speaking of here is defined by you. It could be safe and tame, or wild and radical. When we don't suppress the Spirit, our own perceptions—especially about ourselves—begin to change.

BRAVERY

Following the wisdom of the Spirit and releasing that energy into the world can be really, really scary. It can also be weird. "You're not one of those Bible thumpers are ya?" Just on Sunday between 10:30 a.m. and noon. The rest of the week I'm just a weird Christian. Being weird comes easy to me, but throwing my spirit out there for the world to see … not so much. In my first book, I wrote about some real personal stuff. I was terrified to put it out there. I had some deep conversations with God about exactly what I was putting in that book. I needed to mine a warrior spirit and trust that God had my back, which He did. If you feel deep down in your heart that you're being asked to follow your gut, be brave and sprint now. Move in the direction your gut is guiding you. Get out of your mind and move out of your own way. Fear is a means we use to sabotage ourselves. I'm not saying fear isn't healthy or a good warning sign in many cases, but there's a difference between primal fear and the fear of being different, of stepping outside of your comfort zone. Primal fear indicates that we may be in danger, and it heightens our response mechanisms. Fear of being different or moving into what God may be asking us to do isn't real fear; it's the result of conditioning. It's societal fear.

More than likely we won't be eaten by a predator or squashed by space junk, but we crush ourselves under huge boulders of fear because we feel self-conscious. This fear leaves many goals unpursued. We convince ourselves that this is a real fear. We could die if we express our spirit out there in the scary wilderness of society! Be brave and you'll find that the feedback you get will shred the perception you've created around this unfounded fear. Bravery is actually not that hard; it's harder to live with the regret of not being brave. Courage is within you, and you were designed to be courageous. You have the courage to stand in your truth and live in that truth. Once you step up into your courage, you'll be amazed at how many people will follow you and support your energy.

DESIRE

Desire carries a lot of bad connotations. I'm human, and desire has had its way with me on many occasions. When we desire a Spirit-filled life connected in relationship with God, we should pursue that desire with all of our heart, mind, and energy. When we look at desire in this way, it can change how we perceive the world itself. Desire is a form of pursuit. What we use that desire for is simply a choice. The energy and focus of what we are pursuing can have grave consequences or lead to great success in our Vision. Don't tread lightly when it comes to desire. There are many healthy desires that do not have to lead down the path of sin.

Desire can ignite a fire deep within us that will help us follow and move along the path of our Vision. Desire can unlock the energy of the heart and release it upon your goals and dreams. Channelling the energy of desire, like any other energy, has to be a conscious choice. Desire when unchecked can be blind and lead down paths of ruin or even destruction. Be aware of things you desire and conscious of them pulling you in a direction you know you shouldn't go. Trust in the wisdom of God and ask for His direction. When your desire aligns with your Vision, you'll have a powerful force and energy at your fingertips. Once desire has been awakened, motivation becomes heightened. Don't over-think it or allow that powerful motivation to wane with endless planning; move now and move daily. Don't get paralyses by analysis. which can create a sense of overwhelming indecision.

Pursuing life is a study in desire. Design a set of simple questions you can ask yourself when desire rises up. Is this the right path to follow? Does this feeling of desire align with my values? If I pursue this desire, will it cause harm to others? Simple questions like this can become an auditing habit to help us stay true to our pursuit of our Vision. Desire can be a wonderful human quality with great power. It can rise and fall, and we can spend a long time pursuing something that we truly desire. From the time I started writing my first book until it was published covered a period of nine years. There was a lot of rejection, rewriting, and wanting to quit; however, I endured because the energy from within me was strong. The Spirit stuck with me and pushed me, even when I didn't feel much like continuing. If your desire is strong, you will see it through. Have faith.

Freedom and release from societal conditioning is a great thing to experience. To be free to express doesn't have to be scary or set you up as a target. This freedom was bought with that death on the cross. Racing death is all about moving away from that which will not allow you to be free from death. The life that the death on the cross opened for us is the whole point of pursuing life. Get free in mind, body, and spirit. Pursue with gusto and exuberance the death of a life lived with the intention of gaining God's wisdom.

I read a simple quote the other day, but the author wasn't cited in the work. The quote was simply this: "Quit the life you hate." That's hard to do, but powerful. The best way to quit the life you hate is to give your power over to a higher power. Dig deep inside yourself and get into relationship with the Spirit; don't suppress the amazing energy and love contained therein. Release it, and the world will give you a life you love.

SPIRITUAL RALLY

Are you awake? Are you alive? What will you do today to punch a hole in mediocrity? Start a rally in your life by not allowing the bull of mediocrity to dictate your actions, your energy, or how you choose to live. Mediocrity is the energy that societal conditioning uses to keep the masses from waking up to the full potential of life. It's a lie that helps keep the balance of power in the hands of power-hungry people who don't care about ethical living and the distribution of wealth.

On that hill called Cavalry a spiritual rally was started that we either chose to wake up to or we chose to bury under societal conditioning. At times mediocrity and societal conditioning feel like obstacles we can never overcome. The powers that be have cultivated immense networks to keep this spiritual rally mired in the muck it creates to obscure the truth. You and I have the power every day to free the rally so that those who need it, those who are oppressed and bullied, can experience the freedom of the rally. We who chose to step up for those who need us must face this reality: we will get beaten up and beaten down at times. That's all part of how the rally must unfold. A movement like this has far greater energy and attitude than we can individually carry. Yet take heart, because in your heart is the truth that will set you free from the mediocrity surrounding you. This inner energy that we can rally around is way more powerful than the surface energy that created the mediocrity.

Let's get interested in life ... I mean in real life, way down on an inner level where the crud of society doesn't touch and taint us. The missing link is not missing ... it's just not cultivated enough or expressed in the world. The death on the cross allows us to wake up and truly race death. You're not just a cog in the system. You're a unique entity in the greatest plan ever devised. Wake up to that and rally the power of your spirit. For Christians, this is a battle cry we can carry into our lives every day. I'm not telling you to stand on the corner and scream at people about Christ. I'm not talking about quitting your entire way of living, but taking up the rally of pushing yourself to be the best person you can be within the context of Christian living. Drop the stuff that keeps you from being that person you know you can be. Dismantle the comfort that has been sold to you as a way to live. Open your heart to a spiritual rally that breaks boundaries and destroys non-truth, and you'll experience the ability to pursue a promise of life far greater then we can ever comprehend. Your world is ready to be discovered and explored.

DIVINE SPARK

Here's what I know about spark plugs in a vehicle: they fire in order for the vehicle to start. I have no clue how, or why, they work the way they do. I have no desire to explore or learn the magic of these little devices in my car. I just want them to work when I go to start the car. Up north here in Canada, where I live, it can get cold. In Celsius it can go down below the -30 mark. When it's that cold, you better hope that your spark plugs fire, along with all the other moving parts of the engine.

Let's look at this in terms of our human engine, the spark of our life. When we pursue life, the divine spark inside of us fires daily and lights up the inner energy to face, fight, and forge our way to racing death. When you wake up, your spark is ready to fire. The spark that ignites passion and fire as you work today to pursue your Vision is blowing up the status quo for divine living.

Joy opens a heart to the divine spark in a way that lightens up our life with energy, purpose, and happiness. Is that not a divine spark you want to feel regularly? It doesn't just happen by waiting for the energy to surface itself. A divine spark has to be nurtured and fostered, because it will fade with the world of distraction. Society and our hesitancy to lift each other up combines to snuff out a spark. The prevailing mentality is that we are not going to lift each other up, because it takes a lower energy vibration to tear others down. Competition isn't based on what we can provide, but what we can destroy. People don't actually want to do the work required to build their brand, so they destroy the hard work of others instead.

Our divine spark should always be looking to lift others up and work together to build brands and joy for everyone. When we work this way, the divine spark grows and spreads within us and outwards into the world, creating more opportunity and love. The spirit builds from this spark, and it works hard on our behalf to keep that energy present and growing. Out of the divine spark comes the quality of your true nature, and from that comes your Vision. We pursue life for a reason; the divine spark was not an accident. The joy you experience is a designed way for you to experience what it is that lifts your true nature to the surface. Get fired up and release the power of your nature for the rest of the world to experience!

SPIRIT RUNNER

I'm not a fast or great runner. Sometimes my relationship with running has been a love/hate relationship. Running is one part work, one part pain, and a zillion parts spirit for me. Attitude is huge when it comes to running. I've met so many people on the path who run for different and diverse reasons. Runners are all diverse in their abilities and in how they came to be a runner, but they are all in pursuit of an objective. I run for many reasons. I really started to run because one chapter of my life came to a close, and that allowed for another one to be written. Thirty-two years later I'm still writing that chapter. Not long after I took up running, I realized how healing the activity was for me. I was twenty-two years old and still angry about the injustice done to me as a boy, so when I went for a run, I was running off anger.

Later as I evolved and learned more about what running could do for me, it became about pursuing the spirit. At times in my life depression took me to the lowest depths I'd ever experienced. I wondered if living was really worth it. I hated myself and had no desire to engage in or pursue life. Running became my way to alter and change that energy; it was a release. When I was out running, I'd feel unusual feelings of peace and joy. I was able to connect with nature, even in an urban setting. I started to reconnect with my spirit; I opened up to the connection with God. Actually, I walked through an old door that I'd allowed to close. I ran as far from God as possible as a teen. Now the act of running was bringing me back into relationship with Him.

It wouldn't be until my Ironman in 2004 that the relationship between running and God would be fully illuminated for me. I was and am to this day a spirit runner. Running is my highest level of pursuit and pursuing life. Every run I undertake is a possibility in my life; it makes racing death real. It's a way to break down my self-imposed walls and poor thought patterns and overcome desires. Running builds my spirit and takes me to great places in His wisdom and knowledge.

This same way of thinking and being creates the energy in me to work to inspire and motivate others—the gift God has given me, one I am asked to share with others. Lifting up souls is a wonderful pursuit and challenge. I am blessed to have the opportunity, and it's one I love to follow. It has become part of my spirit running challenge.

RADICAL ENTRY 3

Endurance

" *By your endurance you will gain your lives*" (Luke 21:19, ESV). Alright, how does this whole thing work? I mean, how do we pursue life through God, whom we can't even see? If we are to measure progress and success, it seems that this pursuit has no tangible results. We measure them by the promise of the cross. God promises that we will gain eternal life by pursuing life. In that promise we can chart our whole existence.

We need to be aware of the time factor in life, and that time is an ally on the journey. Trying to force the pursuit will lead us to pursue things that may not be part of our Vision. We can push ourselves into areas that won't help the cause or gain us ground in our Vision. There's a fine balance, and we need to explore different ways as we journey. We need to open ourselves to new things, but how we open ourselves is important. We need to be guided by the inner voice of the Spirit, which will continuously lead us where we need to go. If we are driven by the temptation of desire (and we all will be), we'll stray into some areas that aren't quite where we need to go.

Keep in mind that we are not enduring this alone. Therein lies a great stumbling block that we all face. Too often we rely more on ourselves than we do on God. Pride goeth before the fall. I am acutely aware of this principle in action. Many a time I've been shown by the Spirit ways to work in my life, only to move out with veracity and good intentions but without the presence of the Spirit, because now I'm taking over. I'm going to do this, and I'm going to make it all happen! I often have to take stock a little while later, because I'm not as good at all of this as God is (chuckle).

Enduring through life is an awesome thing. Humans are designed to endure, and through enduring we lift others up. We are not designed for perfection. Excellence is our most enduring pursuit in all we do. Our relationship with God is one of enduring not being able to see Him, yet His presence is our greatest ally in endurance. Doubt is always around the corner, and it's a natural part of enduring. This is the point on the graph that determines whether we continue or not. Doubt is never as strong or as capable as God's wisdom and knowledge. Endure the bad with the knowledge that you are not alone, and everything you require will be provided. Endure the good with a heart of gratitude and remember from whence it all comes—the Hand that created it all. So awesome!

THE MYSTERY OF FAITH

As humans we wake each day to live our lives. We eat, work, play, exercise, and socialize. A common motivator for the average human is to have a long, prosperous life. I think it's safe to say our overall health is something we cherish, as we hope our health will sustain us into our later years so we can enjoy the fruits of our labour. Here is a reality, a truth: our health is based on a lot of hope. We can eat right, exercise, do all the right things currently shoved in our faces daily about how to achieve longevity, but we never have full control over our health.

We endure a lot of things in our lives that impact our overall health. Far too many people experience mental health issues today because of societal constructs. Our society has created unrealistic expectations and values (image, financial, social) that push people out of their natural selves. We become that which we are not in order to become the senseless, mindless, programmed flock we were not born to be. Mental health is and should always be a priority in our lives and in our society.

Comparatively speaking, the mystery of faith in God is no different than the faith to endure all of life's daily stuff for the hope of longevity. People don't question why they endure a job they hate. They don't question why they have to pay so much to live. They blindly pay taxes to governments they don't like without even exercising all of the rights those governments allow. The average person just follows the flock and succumbs to the law of just doing, not living. But they don't see this as a mystery!

The mystery of faith can and will elevate you out of a lethargic, apathetic approach to life. One of the greatest values I've learned in life is that rules don't bind you; rules set you free. We live in a time when people want to break the rules because they feel those rules limit them. In reality, those rules set you free—free to live within a realm of normal day-to-day stability. We require a stable environment to release the true nature with which we were born. Now we are bound by laws and societal rules, which I don't advocate breaking. There will be and are many laws and societal constructs that I abhor. They are part and parcel of living in this society, and I do my best not to break them or cause others pain. The real wisdom that we need to bind us is written in the Word, and that wisdom sets us free.

The mystery of faith lies in the stability of God working behind the scenes in our lives. God would render us all lost and blind if He revealed Himself to us. We aren't capable of processing and handling God in His full splendour. God works in our lives through His mysterious ways, so we cannot allow ourselves to become complacent in our relationship with God. Our comfort zone exists in what we can physically see. Stepping outside of that comfort zone is difficult; we need to change our perspectives or create a new one. Going inside ourselves deeper, searching within our heart to seek God, is the mystery of faith. This is actually more natural to us than relying only on what we see. The mystery of faith is natural. Through natural communication with the creator, we can have an amazing relationship with Him. To experience the mystery of faith is to pursue life and race death by natural habit and nature.

THE SPIRIT/BODY CONNECTION

Have you heard of the mind/muscle connection? In fitness training, great gains are made when an athlete figures out how to get the mind into the muscle. Practises like Tai Chi and Chi Kung are fantastic for learning how to do this. Yoga is another practice that works well for this. The common denominator I have found in all three is the use of breath to really zone in on the practice and gain the benefits. A physical connectivity takes place when athletes train with a focused mind. One can take the energy of the mind and channel it directly into the muscles. I believe that any physical endeavour is 10 per cent physical and 90 per cent mental. Don't confuse the physical I'm speaking of with talent. It takes some level of talent to do any sport or athletic endeavour. Broken down, training for anything is a highly mental process. If you train hard physically, you will always make gains. When you focus the energy of your mind in that training, your overall potential and results increase dramatically; training the mind is essential for athletic competition.

I've been blessed to hang out with a lot of accomplished athletes. The one common denominator I've witnessed in those people is the power of their minds. I've seen so many incredible examples of mind over matter at races and events. Our bodies are designed to go for a long time, with an immense capacity to endure. The mind, on the other hand, will quit. It's weaker and will allow doubt and disbelief to enter. When we take control of the mind through concentrated training, we create a higher connection between the body and the mind.

We have access to an even higher and more powerful connection. The spirit/body connection takes us to a level of performance and living no other connection can compare with.

Or do you not know that your body is a temple of the Holy Spirit within you, whom you have from God? You are not your own, for you were bought with a price. So glorify God in your body. (1 Corinthians 6:19–20, ESV)

Believe you me, I struggle with this scripture daily. We only get one of these bodies, so we should treat it with the utmost respect. Within us is pure energy—energy that created the universe and all we see physically. The spirit which inhabits our bodies is connected to this greater energy. We are connected to the Creator through the mystery of faith by this mind, body, and spirit connection. Every aspect of our being is designed for this spirit connection to elevate us to higher levels of endurance. Through this connection, we learn to enhance the endurance of our mind and not to rely solely on the mind for whatever it is we're facing, voluntarily or involuntarily.

The natural world around us is a conduit to the inner world connection with God. We contain great energy inside of us that we can access and use in our daily pursuit. Our hearts are the key to building and releasing this energy. As an athlete, I use a formula to keep myself training in the right way and to achieve my Vision and my desired results. As a man, I work daily to create this equation in all of my social transactions and dealings—at work, at home, and in my alone time:

$$\text{HEART} = \frac{\text{Mind}}{\text{Matter}}$$

A heart set on an objective, focused on a goal, and filled with fuel from relationship with the Spirit in the temple is the most powerful force we can experience. A heart on fire is an amazing thing to have or witness. It will drive the mind as necessary, and a mind that's directed by such a heart will overcome all matter. Too often we become slaves to our minds, which begin to control and override the heart. This is not the original mind that we're listening to, but a societal, conformist, and impressive mind corrupted by a way of thinking designed to limit us. This mind has been trained since childhood to think in ways that don't cause or create waves. We have been trained to follow the status quo in our mental habits.

The heart is the seat of the Holy Spirit, a guide not impacted by the status quo. When we tap into our heart as the source of our motivation, we become indomitable and natural. This guiding light allows our mind to flow naturally outside of conditioning and with our pure, natural, designed thoughts. This is pure thought, and it comes from the Holy

Spirit and frees us to be who we were designed to be. A heart set on fire by a Vision is the most powerful force in the universe.

This is different from following your heart. When you follow your heart, you base your decisions and path on emotions, bypassing or overriding your connection with the Holy Spirit for quick, emotional satisfaction. How often do we react or act from emotion and then regret it later? When we listen to the Spirit, we are guided and mentored in the knowledge and wisdom of the Lord. That's substantially different than the emotions of the heart. There is great peace and hope to be gained with the connection we have physically to the Spirit. It is far beyond emotion and helps us stay grounded and real in our pursuit.

SPIRIT ENERGY
Pure, powerful, and self-directing energy is ours to access every day and should be what we focus on for our health and wellbeing. It isn't a deep, dark secret we have to search for, either (although there is a lot of value in searching if you know what you want). We are all born with this pure energy and are capable of living a life filled with everything we can imagine by simply aligning ourselves with it. Kingdom living releases us from the earthly struggle of a material and stunted mindset. Radical as it sounds, it doesn't feel radical in the sense of how society defines radical. It feels radical in that we are living from the root of our cause, the design of our Creator.

How do we access this amazing energy? The first step is to simply calm yourself and listen. Constant distraction, escapism, and energy-draining pursuits are deterrents to this wonderful connection. So much of what we face each day is designed to limit and control us so that we don't make the real connection we desire. When we're not connected, we go in search of the next quick fix to make ourselves feel good. We are no longer the masters of our own fortunes, because we allow the connection with the Spirit to be compromised.

Catch a taste of the quality connection with the pure energy of the Spirit, and you will crave more. Pursue this relationship, and it will become a way of life. As we make this our daily bread, nothing can keep us from the Creator. Now we have an immense mentor and passionate

Lord who will show us many amazing ways to fill our heart with passion, love, and joy. Simply set aside time each day to work on this real value, and the benefits will be beyond what you can imagine.

We flirt with mediocrity and get caught in societal crosshairs when we don't pursue this energy—the crosshairs of competing words and actions. The cross fire of values and beliefs. The cross fire of unresolved passions and defying inner energies. We have the ability to stop any confusion and rise above all the uncertainty. Remember what I said earlier about time being an ally in our lives? Nowhere is that truer than in this act of pursuit. Connect with God intentionally by using your time wisely. There's always time for Him. I do this through exercise. My main goal during exercise sessions alone is to be present with God and to listen for the wisdom and knowledge He will provide. I enjoy His company and bask in the enduring love He has for me, and it's there for you as well.

Each day we have a simple choice to make: our true nature versus watered-down reality. Fighting against who we were created to be drains our energy and lives. We create and deal with so much unnecessary stuff that drags us down, but that is a choice. Turn inwards and listen to the wisdom you have written on your heart. Silence the outer world, and a voice will rise up from within you. All of this inner wisdom and the voice have a purpose. They were there the moment you were conceived, designed to move you along a path to serve our creator, who loves you so much that there will never be another person exactly like you. The energy of the Holy Spirit awaits your conscious attention. Build a connection with the Spirit, and you'll never want for true inspiration or motivation.

LIFE

Welcome to your life! As you think, so goes your life. You can be indecisive, wander, flounder, and maybe even get lucky and win the lottery. You can lay blame at the feet of your parents, family, friends, or your boss. If that makes you feel vindicated, good for you ... but it won't change your life. It doesn't matter what age you are at on this journey. Anyone can begin to create a greater life filled with vitality and abundance. Life is a conscious choice; I'm speaking of actual, engaged living. Everyone should get engaged and put all of their energy into that engagement.

Your life is valuable beyond anything you can comprehend. It was bought with a sacrifice of love and a pain beyond what we would endure. The price for your connection to the Holy Spirit was part of a plan for a greater purpose than you just taking up space on the earth. You are so valuable, God asked his only Son to die a merciless death for your salvation. Jesus agreed, even though He could have prevented it. Imagine that conversation between Father and Son: "Son, I have something I need you to do!"

To pursue life in the form of your Vision honours and repays this ultimate sacrifice. Pursuing who you were created to be and then releasing the unlimited energy of your endurance into the world is called purpose. Your endurance is built on an inner desire to live a life filled with love for the earth and all who inhabit it. Pursuing love doesn't just mean with a spouse, family, or friends. It means loving and forgiving your enemy and those who wrong you. It means loving all people and beings. That pursuit takes an enduring spirit. Endurance is not something foreign and outside of us. It's an inner force we can release with willful intent. Build your connection to the Holy Spirit, and you will be able to endure anything. Life is going hurt sometimes and be difficult. You can't avoid all of the pain and suffering life will throw at you, but you can endure it all and come out the other side a much stronger and more accomplished person.

"But the one who endures to the end will be saved" (Matthew 24:13). To me, this scripture screams PATIENCE! Yeah, I know ... patience is a virtue. In essence, patience is morally good behaviour and character. It's connected to the good results that come from something worth waiting for and fighting to achieve. Ok, yeah ... but what does it really mean? When we're pursuing life, we have to patiently wait for all of the hard work and endurance to come to fruition. In this circumstance, patience means to face life with joy in your heart. It's an amazing quality to build into your character, and it will take you further than any education you will ever pay for.

Being impatient is the opposite of enduring. Life is not a spectator sport, and when we feel entitled, we are in for some pain. Your entire being is designed to pursue a relationship with God that will lead to being saved. In the context of the scripture quoted above, you're being asked to endure the life your living for a good cause—your own enduring and everlasting life after your body dies. I like to think of endurance as an opportunity to fully explore the infinite possibilities that God has shown us we can experience.

Life is the only thing we have that is guaranteed. You are the architect of your life, and at any point you can create great works. You choose the great works. You design them and move them to either be realized or not. There's no secret formula to give you the map to achieve your Vision. A great store of endurance resides in your cells, given to you by your Creator so that you wouldn't fail. It's an enduring part of His love, knowledge, and wisdom all tied into a part of you that He knows will rise to the occasion. You must do the work, set the course, and be willing to get gritty in your pursuit.

COMPLETE

> *...when troubles of any kind come your way, consider it an opportunity for great joy. For you know that when your faith is tested, your endurance has a chance to grow. So let it grow, for when your endurance is fully developed, you will be perfect and complete, needing nothing.* (James 1:2–4)

To be complete and to finish the task, to run the race and cross the finish line. What does complete look like to God? I think only He can answer that question. I do know this from my struggles and tribulations faced in this life: there's only one way to be complete. He knew that we would have to endure suffering in the form of sin as we walk our path through life, but His promise to us is that we are not alone. We don't need to rely on ourselves to overcome sin. We are complete when we work daily to be in relationship with and honour God.

Our ability to endure the death of sin is within us, and we are capable of rallying to overcome. It means dropping the conditioning that has led us to believe that there is an alternative path to freedom. Ours is a path of inner endurance, a path lit up bright and energetic when the Spirit entered our hearts to mingle with us and guide us. When we look outside ourselves for the answer to overcoming our human nature, we don't allow our endurance to grow. Trust the guidance you have inside yourself, for it is life itself. To race death, we have a road map, a compass, and an endless supply of water. Life is happening inside of you, so let it flow outwards and into the world where it was meant to inspire and lift up others.

THE CHOICE

If it was easy, everybody would be doing it. We have become reactionary beings instead of action-based beings. Life in societal terms has been laid out in such a way as to dictate how we behave. The parameters we have to follow are dictated to us; we simply react and follow the herd mentality. We have become mindless automatons following the internalized conditioning that drives society. To symbolically buck the system, we point our finger at all the people and circumstances that have made us this way; we have created our own apathy. We drink the Kool-Aid and complain about our results.

THE CHOICE gives you an opportunity to turn the status quo inside out and take back the energy of your true nature. This isn't just a simple act by default of raising your voice in protest then shrinking back into the flow of the status quo. Every person who holds this book in their hands can change the course of history when they decide to make a choice. Your history is worth the time and effort.

If the things happening in your life and the world around you aren't what you want, change them! No one is going to come to your rescue. If they do, you'll need to be rescued again down the river. This is an act of valour on your own behalf, and you're the hero in this story. Write it and live it. Take note now of the excuse popping into your mind and eliminate that thinking and mentality. That thinking has kept you in the energy loop that creates apathy, because you believe that excuse is valid. It needs to be eliminated and exposed for what it truly is—fear. Make the choice right now to see through the fear and its limiting value to the reality of your greater worth and potential.

We choose the endurance path so that we can recreate the truth we're entitled to. We must decide whether to whine and complain, or to shut up and kick butt. Yeah, that's right, to kick butt. Endurance is a choice between being reactionary or becoming a proactive force in your own existence. Life is not and will not always be easy. We have endurance built into our tapestries and can call on that energy at will. Right now we have the choice to dig deep within our own hearts and rise above the chaff. It's your choice. Endurance isn't for the rich or the ones we think are special. You are the special one with the ability to make a choice and open yourself to the greatness you have within.

WORK YOUR WAY THROUGH IT

Uuugh! Work, you say? Let's face it ... sometimes having to endure is hard work and can really suck. Quitting feels like it may be the only option. Well, it's not. Life doesn't have timeouts or halftimes (even holidays don't qualify as these). We're often knee-deep in the muck and only partway across the expanse. Life can really get messy and feel heavy, but quitting is not an option. You can't quit life. People check out and tune out all the time. That's a bad way to approach life. Quitting is dying.

Life has its downs, but when you have a pursuit mindset, you're not going to be impacted as heavily by those downs. It's easy when we're in the up phases of life. Your commitment to pursuit will bring you through when life isn't in full cooperation mode. I get down regularly, don't get me wrong, but I've learned to refuse to allow those moods or events to linger and impact me and my pursuit of objectives.

We can respond to life when it has us down in two ways. We can bury our heads in the sand and hide. Sometimes this feels best and can help for short periods of time. The best course of action, though, is to work your way out of it. Taking action, any action, is a better alternative than moping around and feeling sorry for oneself. The power of even small actions focused on moving toward pursuing your Vision has a profound impact on your overall mood. This takes you from being acted upon to taking action and being in control. When you take action, you change the rules and level the playing field. Small can be really powerful.

Don't over-think or place too much value on taking massive action. Lots of small, incremental actions lead to radical results.

The feeling of control is the objective. You can work daily at creating the energy to overcome all obstacles. That is the essence of endurance. Having absolute belief in your ability to go the distance can become your mindset, and it will make all the difference when the downs hit. Doubts are squashed as you continually work at your pursuit. This kind of control and self-belief serves as a force multiplier for you as a person on a mission. Doubt is a terrible feeling, and when it starts to linger, it's game over. It will rise up for sure; however, the ability to control it through focused action is your advantage. Endurance is built on focused intention and energy.

Work isn't a bad thing; in fact, it's the only thing that will get you to your objectives. Pursuing life is an option; pursuing death is another option. If we want to race death and live a vibrant and energized life, we must be prepared to work. That word isn't only about the work we do to get paid. That's a necessity in life. The work we do in our pursuit is an option but will bring us far greater rewards than any other work with which we fill our time. You can work hard, work smart, measure your work, temper your work, plan out your work, and manage your work, but you should never avoid the work. That will not lead to life.

Lifestyle by Design

Life is a style; we style our way through this amazing gift. Building the lifestyle you desire requires attention and intention. It's a continuous decision to take action on a daily basis to move in the direction you want to be going. It's not perfection … it's dedication. Many "mind weeds" pull us in and trap us in things we think, or believe, we need. They take us off course, divert our natural flow, and blur the inner vision.

The word "lifestyle" contains one of our key words—life! Style is how we want to express ourselves in the outer world. The real work of this expression occurs on the inner landscape of our spirit, heart, and minds. To be in pursuit is to constantly chase after that which we are intent on having, or in creating. Pursuing life is an act of joy, if you so choose to allow yourself that energy. Okay, there's that word—choice. We can choose how our lifestyle will look. We can create it in real time so that we can live it, and we can daily pursue that lifestyle as a means to race death and end up living eternally.

Nowhere in the preceding paragraphs did the word "easy" come up. One of my favourite Ironman bumper stickers states: "If it was easy, everyone would be doing it." That's some of the best advice I've ever seen. Easy is a trap, laid out by advertising and big business to keep you from realizing your true nature and making you believe that there's a magic pill, quick fix approach to everything in life. It's how they keep us buying the stuff we don't need but feel we do because it will make this journey easier. I want to fight, kick, punch, and get bloodied for my lifestyle. That's where the value of pursuing life with every breath comes from, and the end result is the true gold of life.

It's never too late to begin the act of awesomely pursuing life and that Vision. There will be many setbacks along the path (see the chapter on grit). People may not like what you're trying to accomplish and this whole pursuit gig you're embarking on. You can't control that, so don't give it any energy. Explain the objective to people, and if they support you that's awesome. If they look at you with a bewildered expression of incredulity on their face, move on. We pursue life to live at a higher manifestation of our true nature and manage that energy to actually live. Life, good … living dead, bad!

DEFINE IT

In order to live a lifestyle, that lifestyle needs a definition, an outline, and a shape. If our Vision is the essential objective, then our lifestyle is the vessel to take us to completion. In order to aim the available resources and required energy, we need a lifestyle conducive to our main objective. Our lifestyle is not a task to be completed—that just sucks the life out of any pursuit. Our lifestyle is a passion in which we get absorbed, because we created it. When my daughters were younger and in elementary and junior high school, their school had a simple slogan they put on newsletters and other public venues: "Do the little things well." Easier said than done, because in our society the little things are not cool or highlighted. We live in the culture of "bigger is better." When creating your lifestyle and pursuing your Vision, do the littlest of things well, and the big stuff will fall into place. Define the little things that mean a lot to you and then work those into your daily lifestyle. The little things create small building blocks that turn into massive movements in your own life.

Taking some time away from fantastic pursuits such as television, gaming, and any other electronic drain is a great way to start. Defining how you want your lifestyle to look is smart. I understand that fear and trepidation may come to the surface at the thought of actually defining this lifestyle. Maybe you just can't see it. Remember, we're not looking for perfection. Humans are most capable of pursuing life when they're being human beings! I'm big on living as a human being as opposed to human doing ... big difference.

Begin with a broader view of your desired lifestyle as a launch pad and work from there. As time passes, you'll be able to narrow down certain aspects of your lifestyle design. Be open-minded in this part of your design process. Don't over-think this and get caught in the "just thinking" trap rather than acting. Trust yourself and move into places and take actions that speak to your heart. To define this is to define you. That is the power of pursuit in life. You define life, realize it, and take control over that one thing you can control—you!

RITUALS

Creating lifestyle rituals is an awesome way to build the lifestyle you want. Go as far as to schedule these rituals into your day. Making them a priority makes you a priority. There are beautiful, lifestyle-building habits, and then there are negative, lifestyle-draining, dismantling habits. Rituals are habit building super blocks. To establish and maintain aspects of your desired lifestyle helps you to keep them front and centre in your mind. Creating an ally of your mind is key to this process. If we want to create a lifestyle, we need to design it to overcome distraction, confusion, and old conditioning.

Our desire to have a lifestyle that allows us to pursue our Vision can gain great energy and momentum every time we overcome old draining and limiting habits and patterns. That which we have to work really hard for is often the sweetest victory gained. Some parts of creating and designing your lifestyle may be easy, while other parts will be really hard and cause emotional struggle. How badly do you want it?

Let's go back to the scheduling of rituals idea. Schedule the activity you desire to make a habit and then stick with it for an allotted time. Time is on our side when we're working toward designing the lifestyle we desire. Time gives us opportunities to work within the design and build what we see as our Vision. We have more ability to control time than we believe. Your life is your time. Being conscious of how you spend it will help you design your lifestyle by knowing if you are utilizing or wasting your time. Pick a simple action you know you can be successful scheduling into your time and start. When you create a ritual surrounding that one action, you'll feel great and that momentum can be pushed into other actions. It's the compound effect in motion. Once you make one thing ritualistic, it will become second nature. We take control of our design and create abilities by creating these desired habits one by one.

ENVIRONMENT (MIND/SPIRIT)

This is such a beautiful component in our lifestyle design. We have so much control over this area that we let it slip away by allowing our environment to impact and control our minds. Boom! That which should be a slave becomes our master. In no area can our mind's perceptions have a greater impact on our ability to design a lifestyle than in our environment.

There are two important environments separate from our physical environment that can impact us: the environments of the spirit and the mind. These two environments have separate seats in our bodies but are eternally connected and should be integrated. A mind is a beautiful thing to waste, and the spirit is saddened when not known on our human journey. The majority of focus today is on the mind. Life is experienced and filtered through the mind. Societal norms are pumped into our minds to make us functioning, party-toting members of the collective whole. Your mind is important, because it can be manipulated to follow what the status quo wants you to believe. That's why creating a self-sustaining mind is of utmost importance. Becoming a mindful human takes work and sacrifice. Hence the pursuit of creating a mind environment that focuses on your own unique mental needs.

I'm going to use the word "power" here. You posses immense personal power to design a mind you want as opposed to having a mind that is constantly acted upon by outside forces. It's beautiful and enlightening when the light goes on in your mind and takes back your personal power by creating a self-directed lifestyle. You still function in society according to its rules and regulations but remain the unique individual you were created to be. In this mental environment, you function at a higher level of consciousness. You make your decisions based on moral and human-based conscience values. Our mind is incredibly formable at all ages. We don't have to be locked into a way of thinking that keeps us from experiencing the vast opportunities available to an open mind. Getting out of the old mind and into the new is pursuing life for its full value.

Adventure is tuning into the wisdom and knowledge we see in our Vision and then pursuing it in life. Racing death is not a passive, sit-on-the sideline, spectator sport. To race death, we need to jump in with both feet and pursue life as if our lives depended on it, because our lives do depend on it. Creating is in our code. We were designed to create life in a grand scope to release all the gifts and talents we were bestowed with to make the world a better place. That in itself is a worthy pursuit. Death lurks in every non-decision. It loves it when you fear the unknown and decide that it's not worth pursuing life.

Death has no place in life. Pursuit takes death out of the equation by keeping us from prematurely decaying. Age can never be reversed; however, decaying is within our power to control and manage. The choice is simple: control the design of the environment to stave off death and heighten your pursuit. There's radical beauty to this minimization of death by racing like a banshee. The race isn't over until you decide it is. The environment is never set in stone.

BE A PIONEER

To venture into the unknown provides a chance to learn how to master ourselves. Being a follower teaches us to be like others; we become part of the herd. We entrench in ourselves the qualities, values, and beliefs of others. Maybe that's safe ... boring, but safe. You may even be happy with this safety. I'm not here to dictate how you should live ... only you can do that. I'm hoping to inspire and motivate you to truly pursue life on your terms and in you own unique way, breaking new ground in your pursuit.

Becoming a pioneer requires a shift in attitude to embrace racing death; passionless living is a slow death. Pioneers still exist today, and they're looking for new horizons that offer a different life from what the herd follows. They continue to dream in colour and push that dream to their front of mind living ... that dream you think others will judge you for. If you have those feelings, it's time to start racing death.

Design a small activity each day that takes you out of your comfort zone. Create a daily adventure on a new path, like a pioneer setting out in search of a new land or a new life ... a new way, and a whole new possible opportunity to live the dream. Give yourself permission to be scared in your pursuit, because it's better than a decaying lifestyle. As a pioneer, you'll meet resistance, both internal and external. Understand that and embrace it. As a matter of fact, it may be extremely uncomfortable. Good! That's because it means so much to you. The minute you take action, you shift the energy.

Once you create this shift in your energy, the place of comfort within you will scream and panic. It can't handle the unknown, and it's terrified of change. To pioneer means looking that fear square on and moving anyway. As a pioneer, you don't care; you only see your Vision. Live the curiosity of a pioneer with every new experience and insight. Each new step along the path is another piece of the puzzle, a part of building your new way—a new mindset and attitude, a new perspective of your inner world that will be expressed in the outer world as you walk in your Vision.

Pioneering means pursuing life and looking death right in the eye while laughing and racing. Pioneers are on the lookout for the deep, inner connections that blow up the status quo and free them from the barriers of lies. As pioneers, we create the way we live in every detail to ensure that we are not denying our true nature. Being a pioneer is a statement in life, a statement that death has no place in your mindset. To move out of a system of dying because of a lack of ambition is being a pioneer. Pioneering is signing the document of your life with an attitude of not settling for anything less than living your Vision.

ATTITUDE

You should have an attitude, one that defines you within your set of beliefs and values. It takes a unique way of thinking to define a lifestyle today. So much information is directed at us about *how* to be, do, walk, live, talk, dress, and conform. You either accept those beliefs, or you open your mind to the inner dimension available to help you transcend the lies. Life wasn't meant to contain your greatness or suppress your spirit. Designing an attitude isn't about being rude, stand-offish, or ignorant. It means not settling for what others or society say you should. To transcend a boring or conformist path takes work and energy. I guarantee that at times this is a lonely path. It's lonely because it's worth it.

You want an attitude that never says die. That Vision is worth fighting for and keeps you moving. It's the ultimate pursuit point. Create your attitude to align your life with this pursuit point. Create the thoughts, actions, and energy to live your Vision. This attitude is about being indomitable. Attitude is not a negative vibe if you're passionate about your Vision and are not harming others as you walk; then your attitude is a tool to help you make your way.

The energy of a "can do" attitude is not only contagious, but it infuses you with the personal power to live it out loud. An attitude like this may rub some people the wrong way. Don't intentionally be abrasive; be intentionally focused on tasks you need to accomplish. Tell people what you intend to do. You're being honest, and if they can't handle that attitude, so be it. Your attitude needs to be flexible. It doesn't need to make you submissive. Make no excuses about your Vision and what you want to achieve. Put your full energy into a lifestyle designed to achieve the end result, the pursuit point.

PROCESS

Process is an amazing thing to be in, but a hard thing to follow. We have the ability to design our lifestyle through process, taking a systematic series of actions so that at the end of that process we become what we want and intended. The challenge is to set the process and then follow it through to the end. Essentially, we're always in the process of something. The question is whether we are in command of that process, or if it's stealing our lunch money! There's a really big difference. We're either being proactive and designing our lifestyle through a process, or we're in the constant process of just reacting to what life throws at us. Life often has a way of kicking our behinds if we're not taking the lead.

This is a "to do" book. When it comes to creating process that allows you to explore building blocks for your lifestyle, get out there and explore! Make conscious efforts to explore activities and avenues that will enhance your desired lifestyle. Get off of the beaten path and do some bushwhacking. There are surprising options out there. I've found it helpful to keep a journal. Journaling is a record-keeping habit that helps record your history. You can always go back over your history and discover little bits of information that will guide, affirm, clarify, and help you create a process that works for you. Journaling can also open your mind to finding new ways of living in the process you are designing.

When in process, you can consciously design actions, moments, maps, and any circumstances you want. You choose how this moment of this day will impact your objective. Process is either intentional or it is reactive. You want to be in the process of personal control. You may not be able to change your circumstances, but you can gain a lot more control … the kind of control that allows you more personal power over those circumstances. That kind of power is life-altering and leads to change on the inside. Once you start that process of change, creating more and more change in your life becomes possible. The more process you create, the higher your rate of return will be.

The process of elimination is a good way to understand what does and doesn't bring value and worth to your pursuit. I recommend trying it out. Try anything you think will benefit your pursuit. Maybe it has value, and maybe it doesn't, but at least you'll know, because you tried. Maybe the weirdest, wackiest ideas will turn into gold for you and become a part of your process. Life is a process of elimination as you move along the path of your choice.

BUILDING A GOOD STRUCTURE

On a personal level, I embrace paradox in many areas. I believe in chaos theory and nature. In order to successfully pursue our Vision, we need a strong structure. Are you confused yet? Structure is good for energy. The foundation of pursuit is the energy to continually move in the direction of that Vision.

Structuring our lifestyle on our own terms is less restrictive than societal structure and less energy draining. Being controlled by structure isn't healthy, especially when we have no say in that structure. That's why it's essential to build your own structure into life as a means of control. You're not being selfish when you work at creating a structure that helps you be a better, happier, self-fulfilling person. Be aware of what you need, and then move to create that kind of structure in your life.

Structure your day in ways that allow you to focus some time on actions that will allow you to pursue your Vision. Structure is a great way to build peace into our lives. Energy is constantly in motion and flux, which is a good thing. To take that energy and structure it is to harness the absolute power contained in that very energy. You are that energy; it's one and the same. The Creator made everything in our physical realm out of the same energy. We flow with, in, around, and through it all of the time. It can be wild and unruly, and it can be structured and powerful. Both have immense value and benefits.

WHAT IS RELEVANT?

Our goal should be to focus on what's relevant for our designed lifestyle and then apply those key things to our lives. Time is finite, so wasting time in pursuit of non-relevant things is not cool. It's a waste of energy. It's time we'll never get back. Wasting time moves us harmfully away from pursuing our Vision, so we must ensure that we focus on relevant things. I'm not talking about exact science here; however, there should be some personal science involved.

Science is the systemic study of the physical and natural world using observation and experiments. We should be scientists, observing and experimenting on ourselves. To train for and compete in an Ironman Triathlon was similar to performing a science experiment on myself. There is much science involved in training and preparing for this event, allowing the athlete to go into the race with a clear picture and structure in place that will help them to succeed. They have eliminated what isn't relevant and incorporated what is.

Work hard to determine what's relevant to the success of your pursuit, as this will help you succeed. Sounds redundant, I guess, but it's true. The truth doesn't vacillate; the truth is reality and will always bear witness. This is really a "feel" thing. We sense what feels right and what feels wrong. Too often, though, we don't listen to our true feelings to determine what's relevant or irrelevant. We should always consider our own feelings, and especially our gut feelings, first.

It's easier to understand what's relevant once you gain an understanding of your Vision. The desire to get away from what doesn't feel right is a signal. We have that feeling for a reason and need to trust it. At different stages of your pursuit, what's relevant for you will change. As you master certain aspects of yourself and practices, they'll no longer require your focused energy. Move on from them without feeling bad. We tend to hold on to what was once relevant because it was comfortable and known, but if it's no longer benefitting us, it needs to be removed. Don't hold on to things just for the sake of comfort.

INTEGRATE

I've arranged this book into different chapters and headings. I find that breaking it down into smaller chunks makes it easier to understand. Like a jigsaw puzzle, it's easy to find the border outline pieces because of their straight edges. Get the outline done and then fill in the centre or integrate all of the pieces to make the puzzle. In our Western culture, we tend to separate ourselves into different components and pieces. We separate aspects of our lives into different sections, different caves within ourselves, and we segregate these pieces from other pieces; however, we are all of the labels we carry, and they all make up a whole person. All of them are a part of us, and we need to treat them all with love and respect.

In this book I share the things I've integrated into my life to create the lifestyle I desire to achieve my Vision. I integrate the smaller ideas and information into what I consider to be the whole me. I work hard to unite all that I am so that I am in pursuit of life. We need to stop judging ourselves by the unrealistic portrayals presented in the media and television that bombard us regularly.

We must always work to minimize our impact on our environment and those around us. Taking responsibility for this is called accountability. In being accountable, I freely accept all aspects of myself, which frees up energy to work on creating change. I can now improve my abilities to prevent society's messages from impacting my life adversely. I'm free from the perceived negative energy and can flow in all the areas I want to increase my efforts toward my Vision. Integrate all your energy into one common goal for you. Allow that energy to move freely through your pursuit and embrace all aspects of who you are. I describe myself as a Daniel energy bomb. I'm blowing up the conditioning that limits me and moving freely into my Vision, all integrated as a work in progress.

TRAIN TO BE CONSISTENT

The alarm goes off at some ridiculous hour and they jump out of bed. They're tired, don't kid yourself, but that workout or whatever they're getting up for is too important to sleep through. They know that by doing this, they're going to feel better; they'll feel a sense of accomplishment. They have built the act of being consistent into their lifestyle. Many of the people I know who succeed in their fitness goals, who compete in Ironman, Ultramarathons, and other amazing things, are consistent in their actions and lifestyle. They understand that achieving their objectives requires them to build habits that will ensure they succeed.

Creating consistent pursuit patterns brings better results than just winging it, and it also helps with energy management. When we first create a new habit, it takes energy and focus to become consistent. Over time, we assimilate this new habit into our lives and it becomes second nature. We learn to love these actions, because we've made a conscious choice to be consistent in them; they are part of our plan for mastery. We feel a far greater sense of personal control over our own emotions and life. Consistency reduces the impact of outside forces by building up spiritual immunity to them.

When we create positive pursuit patterns, we equalize the equation. Taking the dull, mediocre edge off of life is simply a matter of being more edgy yourself, standing out there at the edges of the status quo and saying, "I'm not buying that." It takes a consistent pursuit to not be a member of the herd.

Begin small; pick one action you really want to create as a positive pursuit pattern and be consistent in it for thirty days. Don't allow excuses to creep in and undermine the consistency. Maybe you need to set your alarm. That's what sets you apart—you're not into the status quo. Build a habit of consistency into your lifestyle. You're worth the time and effort. Everyone you love is worth the time and effort. Over time, the effort will return immense benefits and inner peace for you and the environment you occupy. Consistency will open space in you to receive the gifts of energy and joy that you deserve.

GRATITUDE

For a great deal of my life I've been pessimistic, negative, and ungrateful. Being ungrateful created a massive energy block in my life. I didn't see how much I had to be grateful for; instead, I focused on all I didn't have and laid the blame on my past. I was dying; my energy was being channeled into pursuing death. I wasn't happy with myself or anything happening in my life. I was a lost soul on what should have been an amazing journey that I could be creating on a totally different level.

I needed to develop an attitude of gratitude. It would take work, effort, and energy to turn around my negative framework. I looked at my life and saw how good I had it. I needed to shift my perspective and stop feeling sorry for myself. I wasn't racing death ... death was at my doorstep, and I was willingly opening the door. I had to learn to live right here and right now and focus on the good stuff.

When I started to measure my life, I found a lot to be grateful for. In the battle of life, I was losing where it matters the most—between the ears. My mental fitness was low and bringing me bad mental energy. I needed to make a conscious choice to change my perspective and focus intentionally on all I had to be grateful for. I had to make the effort to deliberately practice gratitude.

I learned that gratitude is easier than pessimism. From an energy standpoint, it takes way less energy. The return is vibrant energy that is healthy and a game changer. By creating optimism through gratitude, my mental energy shifted to a new dimension. Fighting with life because of a negative perspective is draining. On the flip side, waking up with a heart filled with gratitude creates uplifting energy. Gratitude is key to mastering anything, and your pursuit of mastery will accelerate with gratitude working for you. A mindset of gratitude allows us to see opportunity in all areas of life. We are alive and can make a dent in the universe by mastering the attitude of gratitude.

Drawing a Conclusion

After publishing *Nobody Can Take It Away from You*, I sought and received feedback about the book. I'm always looking to improve upon my work, and any kind of feedback will help me do that. The main idea for this book was already in place, so I was moving along the writing timeline and getting others' perspectives. I already knew what I'd do differently with the second book. Let's face it, seeking feedback—especially in the form of constructive criticism—can be difficult; however, I'm a big boy and in order to improve the creative process, it was necessary.

For some people, giving feedback can be difficult. If they didn't like the work, it can be hard to be honest. People generally don't want to hurt other people's feelings. Constructive feedback doesn't come naturally to some. In this politically correct world, one can suffer serious backlash for openly critiquing. I'd start my spiel soliciting for feedback by asking people to be honest, as I could take the negative if they were being honest. Even then I could sense that some people weren't fully opening up with me. Fortunately, I did get a lot of constructive and helpful feedback. Some quality ideas came from people who generally felt that they're not that creative.

I DON'T BELIEVE THERE HAS TO BE A CONCLUSION

A couple of people with strong backgrounds in writing and production felt that *Nobody* didn't draw a conclusion. In their minds, I didn't give the reader a completed ending, a closing formula. It was good feedback and something I pondered for quite some time. *Nobody* took a portion of my life to the end point of that portion. I've always described *Nobody* as autobiographical but incomplete, because I'm still doing what I do. I wrote *Nobody* as an inspirational piece to capture my first Ironman race and describe how it brought me fully back into relationship with God. I wanted to show people how that process led to healing for me, and I hoped it would help them in their relationship with God. I guess in my mind it was very conclusive.

How should I approach this book? Do I need to be more aware of nailing down a conclusion? I thought about the process of beginning with the end in mind. Well, I always do that anyway. I began by writing the last chapter first and then contemplated writing the rest of the book in reverse. Writing the last chapter first gives me the ability to work toward the solid idea of the book in my mind, and then I can always adjust, add, subtract, or build upon that final chapter.

As I looked at this present work, I didn't feel like a conclusion was a make or break deal. I intend to inspire and motivate people, to get them to move and live. If I provide a conclusion based on my way, then they may have read the book for nothing. They may not be able to relate to my conclusion.

A MATTER OF STYLE

The process began by stepping back to examine why I write. Writing *Nobody* proved to be a cathartic and healing experience for me. I always said that if the book helped one person, then it was worth it. I had one person who was struggling with an addiction in their lives tell me that the book made a difference for them. That was the entire conclusion I required for my purpose.

It all comes down to a matter of style. My goal again is to inspire and motivate. If I'm not moving the needle of my energy on the path God has shown me, then I'm being selfish and doing things for my own end game. Ultimately when writing a book, the author should feel good about it when it's completed. My goal is to ignite a fire in the reader to move out of things that are not helping them to fully pursue life.

Provoking someone to move and chase after their dreams, or race down a goal, is the greatest joy I feel in my coaching and writing. I love it when someone sets out to accomplish something and they see it through. Hey, maybe they even have an unrealistic goal in the eyes of societal conditioning, which I'll get behind with an even fiercer energy. If I write something that pushes a button that starts someone down a path without a clear conclusion, then I'm successful.

My style isn't about conclusions. Every day is an opportunity for us to move the needle in the direction of our objectives. This book is about pursuing life on your terms, in your unique way, with your conclusion as the end goal. You define it. My objective is to pursue life to the fullest as I define it. Coming to a conclusion can sometimes lead to a closed mind. Run without a destination in mind.

THE FORMULA

Here's the secret formula: it doesn't exist. That is, it doesn't exist unless you create it for yourself. If you build it for your own unique path, then you'll succeed. The ideas I share here may help you or provoke you to think differently or move in a different way. For me to think that everything I write here will work for you would be naïve. Your formula will be different from mine.

Become a scientist in your life. Devise a hypothesis and test it. Experiment with the things you feel may be of benefit, and then decide after experimenting with them if you'll continue to use them. Step out of the things that you know for sure aren't working. Write a new formula, but don't write it for perfection.

I've wasted copious amounts of time looking for the magic bullet formula with the hopes it would turn my life around. I found many valuable tools that helped me create some change and improve my pursuit lanes, but I wasted a lot of time. There is no magic bullet formula, but we do have access to real wisdom and knowledge. I'll leave you with this formula: you are alive. That is the truth. You are amazing, and that is the truth. Your unique energy will never be subdued if you don't allow it to be, and that is the truth. Your formula is written on your heart.

THE OLD FORGONE CONCLUSION

We've all heard it ... the "you shouldn't follow that path" speech. "You're much more suited to do this; follow this path." (As a parent, I did this at times.) Teachers, guidance counsellors, and others have tried to give us advice about what we should do. Yes, the old foregone conclusion. How many times have we failed to try because it seemed as though it was a foregone conclusion? Maybe we didn't apply for that job because we didn't have the credentials. We chose not to attempt that risky opportunity, because "they never work out for me."

Before even taking a chance, we often come to the foregone conclusion. In reality, maybe it's easier not to try than to try and fail. Life doesn't have to be filled with foregone conclusions. History is filled with champions who were told they didn't have a chance to win, because it was a foregone conclusion. Those champions didn't listen to reason; they believed in themselves. Nothing in the theory of possibility is a foregone conclusion. The minute we accept the foregone conclusion, we put a limit on ourselves. Yes, we need to be realistic. But to give something a value that isn't real is being unrealistic. The foregone conclusion is accepting a death of small proportions; the more of these we accept, the closer to death we really come. Living dead is a conclusion that comes from the foregone conclusion.

THE ALTERNATIVE ENDING

Many movies on the big screen these days have an alternative ending. Maybe the director didn't like the original conclusion, so they decided to film a second one. Maybe the screenwriter felt having two options made for a better process in the filming. It could be that the current movie-going crowd isn't satisfied with just one option, yet some of them will settle for only one conclusion of their life. And often that conclusion is a long-ago-decided forgone conclusion.

Too often we settle for a conclusion we believe is best for others, but it's not in our best interests. Sometimes we stifle our dreams and our Vision because to pursue them might mean being judged by others. So many great works have never been completed because of forgone conclusions of failure—not because it wasn't possible, but because the creative energy of the individual was suppressed by societal conditioning. Nothing is foregone if we decide we're willing to pursue it

PURPOSEFUL CONCLUSIONS

How about we just write our conclusions with purpose fuelled by passion and wonder? This is the possible tipping point in our own journey and can create a new way to pursue. With intention we can create all the conclusions we see as important. This takes work, and we'll encounter obstacles. Unfortunately, we're often afraid that we can't achieve our conclusions. Excuses pop up, and we give ourselves an out. It's always easy to find things that are working against us.

This is where grit comes into play. To pursue life means that sometimes you just have to suck it up and deal. Life isn't fair, and you better learn how to deal with it. GRIT UP and really know for sure what our purposeful conclusions are. We aim for volume instead of quality. If we diffuse our own energy over massive amounts of conclusions, we'll have no energy for the valuable ones. We have immense potential and extreme capabilities within us when our focus is set on purposeful conclusions. Discipline becomes a laser-focused beam of energy.

THE NEVER-ENDING CONCLUSION

I've often experienced the high of achieving the finish line of major athletic goals. The sense of accomplishment, success, and the sheer rush of being alive are tremendous. It never gets old, but there can be a real emotional and mental crash at the conclusion of a big event. After my first Ironman in 2004, I crashed hard mentally. It was a bit scary to feel how heavy that could be, so I chose after that to never have a conclusion.

Our true goal, the race we're running in and all of our training, are for a never-ending conclusion. The conclusions we settle for aren't the real ones we should be pursuing. There's only one conclusion we should pursue ... all others along our path either lead to or away from that ultimate conclusion. Be diligent in what conclusions you pursue, as your end conclusion depends on it.

"Enter through the narrow gate. For wide is the gate and broad is the road that leads to destruction, and many enter through it" (Matthew 7:13, NIV). The gate of self-destruction is wide, and there are many, many ways one partakes of it. We can have all the excitement and joy the pursuit of life can offer as long as we're responsible in our intentions and keep our focus on the narrow gate. That narrow gate is the ultimate conclusion. Learning to monitor our thoughts and behaviours so we see ourselves at that gate is the great purpose of our pursuit. So much personal pain and suffering can be removed from our lives by fully pursuing this narrow gate. Any conclusion that doesn't have you in pursuit of the gate takes you down the wrong road.

POWER

This is a scary word. Power isn't a bad thing in itself. What's done with it is what counts. Power of the personal kind comes from one essential quality we all have: character. People define us by our character, and we all have the power to define our character. We can mould our character no matter how old we are or at what stage we find ourselves in life.

Serving others is a great character builder and a true test of character. To hold a position of power and serve others increases your power. Power shouldn't be abused, but routinely it is. When you see your position as a launching point to create for others, you're being a servant. This isn't a bad thing or in any way demeaning. To serve others is true power. We free ourselves when we create a servant's heart. This kind of power is generated by knowing our Vision, which is designed from our heart truth. You can't pursue life or your ultimate conclusion if you don't have personal power, which is the ability to know your Vision and seek the conclusion that Vision shows you. This power doesn't allow the world to take from you that to which it has no right. This power comes from your spirit and connects to the highest level of self-knowledge available.

OKAY, HERE IS A CONCLUSION
In conclusion, go out and get it!

RADICAL ENTRY 6

Grit

Angela Duckworth is what you'd call an expert in the study of grit. In her TED talk, "Grit: The Power of Passion and Perseverance," Duckworth defines grit as passion and perseverance for long term goals. Grit means having stamina and sticking with your future, day in and day out—not just for the week, not just for the month, but for years, and working really hard to make that future a reality.[1] In another place, Duckworth states: "What we accomplish in the marathon of life depends tremendously on our grit—our passion and perseverance for long-term goals."[2] Grit means living life like it's a marathon, not a sprint.

I love it, try to live it, and have some totally messed up days when I'm my own biggest enemy and fool. AAAAAAGGGHHH! But I love it! I'm uncertain at times about my own ability to grit it out, but I continue to learn and grow. In certain areas of my life, I'm off the charts when it comes to grit. I can look at my bucket list and see a great deal of it accomplished. Some things continue to come up and I work toward them, but I have a lot of check marks in the proper columns. But I still want to be grittier, more passionate about this beautiful thing called life.

---

[1] Angela Lee Duckworth, "Grit: The Power of Passion and Perseverance," filmed April 2013, TED video, 6:09. https://www.ted.com/talks/angela_lee_duckworth_grit_the_power_of_passion_and_perseverance

[2] Angela Lee Duckworth, *Grit: The Power and Passion of Perseverance* (New York, NY: HarperCollins, 2016), 269.

Can grit be the difference between pursuing life and simply bearing it? I think there's a correlation between a grit attitude and the comfort zone. Being in the comfort zone diminishes grit. I've observed this in many people. If comfort has been provided to you in every aspect of your life, how hard is it to really dig deep when the going gets tough? Think about this for a minute. How hard did your ancestors have to work so that you could have this level of comfort? How lucky were you to be born into this level of comfort? I know for myself I didn't have to work that hard when I was young for my comforts.

The majority of people reading this will have been born into a relatively comfortable lifestyle. To those of you who had to forge out a lifestyle of comfort through grit and determination, I tip my hat. The majority of us must remember that someone before us had to work so that we could experience this lifestyle. Their grit is the reason we have what we do, either directly or indirectly. Don't fool yourself and believe that you're entitled to what you have. You're entitled to build your own level of grit to pursue life.

Much of what we pursue in life is materialistic comfort. We work long hours just to reach a point of retiring financially secure. Hopefully we get there with our health! The status quo states that our lives are completed by the material possessions we deem necessary to survive. Daily grinds, bills, the state of our homes and yard—these are the things that have come to define us as a society. This societal conditioning works hard to take us out of our natural rhythms so that we become the wandering herd. The current system is designed for us to be assimilated into it for its purpose rather than for us to be self-actualized and free.

Grit isn't just the stuff of Hollywood or what the mainstream media feeds us. Grit was born on a cross, and the opportunity for us to live it is a choice we were all given. The foundation and example for us to live a life of grit was set by a man who chose the ultimate sacrifice for us. Here is the beauty again—we can choose to make that connection and forge the same kind of grit in our own lives. We all have experiences—some good, some bad—but if we're fortunate, we'll experience a whole lot of great. All of life's lessons, humiliations, triumphs, and boring moments have forged each of us. Boredom is a great builder of grit. It gives you an opportunity to dig inside of yourself and discover what's really happening. Distraction is not the cure for boredom... the pursuit of that Vision you have for life is.

It's natural for us to gravitate toward happier experiences and live from the more positive emotions we experience. Feeling good and not experiencing negative vibes and emotions is healthy. We try to design our lives through the accepted norms to control factors that make us uncomfortable, or even eliminate any negative personal challenges. No matter how much we try to avoid pain in this world, it will come. If you're not prepared for this aspect of life, then you're going to really struggle because it all can't be good. Not to worry—you have the ability to turn it all into a super-charged energy to not only pursue life to its fullest, but to excel in grit.

We can learn, develop, enhance, and teach grit. I've been blessed to hang out with some gritty, crazy, obsessed, and totally awesome people. They are athletes, parents, fathers, mothers, husbands, wives, and explorers. They are just like you. The one thing they all have in common is that they're willing to pursue life full on without holding back.

THE OBSTACLE

God is equal to or above mind over matter. Life itself is an obstacle. We face death in many ways. Our current lifestyles have created so many health issues, it's a tad bit scary. Cancer and diabetes are still on the rise. We have longer life spans due to medicine and technology ... but has the quality of life increased? A long time ago I made a choice. I don't have to like everything that happens to me, but I also don't have to let it determine my mindset. Have I perfected this mindset? Not even close. Having the choice to make it though is a difference maker in my pursuit of my Vision.

Life presents obstacles, but our perceptions of these obstacles determine whether we succeed or fail. When we feel desperation, despair, or powerlessness, we've allowed our perceptions to take over. Realistically we have the ability to feel empowered, opportunistic, and alive with every obstacle we encounter. How we decide to approach and live with those obstacles can dictate our lives. I'm going to go so far as to say that as a society we've tried to eliminate obstacles. We're surrounded by legislation and rules designed to remove obstacles along the path.

We need to learn that life isn't fair. As a matter of fact, sometimes it will kick you in the teeth. Life can leave you bleeding, broken, hurt, and wandering. That's when the magic happens... if we've been taught to be accountable and take responsibility for who and what we are. This is where grit kicks in and we kick life right back in the backside. Work harder, work smarter, learn to practice deliberately, and make the outcome different. Try your best and love yourself no matter the outcome on the scoreboard. Be happy that you're able to play.

Obstacles will produce one of two scenarios: either we quit, or we decide that there's no way the obstacle will stop us from pursuing our Vision. We decide that the pain of the obstacle is worth the lesson on the other side, and we take up the challenge and move into the pain. Take the pain to make the gain. If the obstacle defeats us, what can we take away from the defeat? That's the lesson we decide to learn. Remember, there's no formula I can give you for all of this, but I've experienced this myself and seen in many others: you are capable of being gritty and overcoming any obstacle. No matter the outcome, you will be much stronger, more capable, and grittier than if you'd packed your bags and gone home.

CALL IT WHAT IT IS

Pain and hurt are real—let's get that out there in the open and be real about it. Only one person can be the class president. Only one person can be the captain of the team. Someone will be better skilled, more talented, prettier, stronger, and richer ... the list is endless. Are you willing to let that stop you? No one can out-grit or out-work you if you decide to make it happen. That's the choice we have to make. Do we allow those things out of our control to determine how we will live our lives? Grit says no way. Grit is the great equalizer. When all is said and done, if we play with grit and work hard, we can walk away from whatever situation saying "I did my best." My best may not always be enough, but I'm alright with that. That's a truth I can't control, but I can sure as heck control the way I come into any situation. Grit is buildable; we can learn it, grow it, shape it, and then teach it to others.

You're going to get knocked down. How many times are you willing to get back up? Some people aren't going to like you for what you're trying to accomplish. It's better to have tried and not succeeded than to have quit and taken the easy way out.

Life is what it is. We live in a society that manipulates the facts for its own self-serving purpose, but we can choose to try. When we do, we gain the skills that become tools available to us. These tools help us create strategies to face things that will try to hinder our progress. If we continue to build more skills, we'll progress steadily beyond the limiting obstacle to where we want to be. We'll be able to surmount those obstacles that try to keep us from our Vision. Grit is filled with resiliency, the ability to take a hit and keep coming back. Being resilient is the ability to see the value in any setback and make it beyond that point to the next point. Call it what it is— opportunity to grow and become stronger in all areas of our own lives.

THE BIG QUESTION

Am I better today than I was yesterday?

The mindless day after day grind sucks. I see that pain as people have lost the ability to pursue life because of the lure of the comfort trap. Our bellies are over full, we face little or no danger to make us stay fit, and our minds and bodies are decaying. But apparently we have a better standard of living than our grandparents. I'd take their lives over ours any day. My grandparents were way tougher than I'll ever be, but I'm going to seriously try to match their level of grit and living.

I've learned to question everything, most importantly myself. I really don't want to get to the end of the road and look back, wondering what could have been. To be successful in pursuit we need to develop a performance mindset, which is why we need to ask this question every day. That's how we build grit, learn, and grow. If we're not willing to look at ourselves through questioning, how are we expecting to learn?

By asking the big question, my mind seeks different lanes of pursuit for my Vision. (Lanes of pursuit are activities and actions we identify to help us pursue our Vision.) Keeping the same lanes of pursuit throughout our lives leads to mental and spiritual starvation. I want to improve on my yesterday and create even better in my tomorrow. When I open my mind to these different lanes of pursuit, I find new energy and become more exuberant for my Vision. I'm going to find mental lanes of pursuit that work for me and take me out of my comfort zone. Paralysis by comfort is a disease in our society that keeps many people from realizing their amazing potential. Asking if we're better today creates an easily measurable benchmark for our lives.

PAIN

I belong to a group called the P-TEAM. We were three village idiots that got into endurance sports when they were fledgling events. The P stands for pain, and our motto was: "Take the pain." There are two types of pain. The first type signals that it's time to stop; there's something wrong. Then there's the good pain, the type of physical pain you get from effort. We feel this pain because we're working hard physically and our bodies know it. Our effort hurts. It's hard to keep going. At this point, we need to mentally and spiritually dig down deep inside ourselves in order not to quit. We rise up in our hearts and keep pushing through the pain. We don't allow our minds to focus on the pain; that is the grit of endurance.

Pain is real. It can be physical, mental, emotional, or spiritual. You can never avoid all the pain of life. All the people you follow on social media have perfect lives ... right? A life without pain is simply impossible. Life doesn't discriminate when it comes to pain and who feels it.

When you set your mind on a path of pursuit, pain will be a companion at some point. The true visionary pioneer will have some really painful days. The path may be lonely, but people who are willing to wander in the desert or wilderness know what it takes. These people are patient and persistent, even in the face of pain. People who don't, who won't, be patient will find that their Visions never get off the ground.

CHASING PAIN

Experience is a great teacher. It's not just a great equalizer, but a difference maker. As I mentioned before, pain doesn't discriminate, and neither does experience. Experience isn't biased, and it rarely plays favourites.

It's there for all who seek to find it in their way and for what their Vision demands. Experience is a willing participant in our lives. To pursue life full on is to seek experience and want the opportunity to create experience. Chase pain, and it will give you experience and a different perspective than if you avoid it at all costs.

Associate with people who love to chase pain, people who aren't afraid of pain or shy away from it. I'm blessed to hang around with people who chase pain and help me push my boundaries and expand my pain threshold. These friends and companions push the limits, feed the experience, and enjoy the outcome that pain can provide. I'm referring to physical pain through endurance racing and training. We don't do this "just because." We do it because we realize that on the other side of that training and racing, pain is freedom—freedom from the status quo and societal conditioning. Be a willing participant in what pain can teach and chase the lesson. That's what pain can offer if you'll look for ways to use it rather than complain and throw a pity party.

THE TRUTH

We all struggle with our own truth on some levels. We know what we want to change, and we understand how much happier and more effective we'd be. Our lives may change a little or drastically by facing the truth. For some reason, we seem unable to be totally honest with ourselves regarding this truth. We are human; we struggle, and that's a reality. One day we may succeed, and the next we fall flat on our faces. The truth can set us free, and the truth can haunt us mercilessly. We sometimes feel off balance when we're in the middle of a truth struggle. The test is real; there is no score to be kept. We are alive and in pursuit, so focus on that as a means to challenge the truth you're struggling with. I could try to define this truth in some way, but I believe it's different for everyone. This truth is the struggle to change on some level as a human.

I find that being absolutely truthful with myself about the situation is the best remedy for moving the needle; the truth will set you free. I have to be honest about it or it will never change. If we can't call the issue what it is and recognize the power it has, how can we change it? Often it's more comfortable to just stay within the comfort zone. Stepping into

63

the truth and changing it initiates the flight response. Certain things about this simple comfort zone drive us crazy, but it's so familiar, we just accept it, even when we want the other option.

Being gritty means knowing that choosing the other option will be uncomfortable but accepting the discomfort as part of the process to move into what is desired. It's easier to change the plain truth than live the elaborate lie. Grit gives you the energy and upper hand in the battle.

Want to experience joy? Tell yourself the truth about that thing you know is causing the inner struggle. Be full on honest about the fact that it bugs you and you don't like it. Allow yourself to get ticked off about whatever it is and the reasons for it. Then stop making excuses and grit up to the change bar. Because when you face the truth, it will set you free. This is true in any area of your life. Racing death is not going to be the casual, sing-song camping adventure we always hoped for.

THE PATH OF LEAST RESISTANCE

The path of least resistance may provide quick and easy results, but not lasting results. I know this from experience. I've tried this path on occasion and found that the results rarely lasted when it came to anything of value. It's never easy to achieve the lasting goals or changes we're looking for. The pursuit of life brings much resistance. I'm thankful for that resistance and what I have learned from it.

Society generally seeks the path of least resistance, so it's easy to adopt the herd mentality. The cure for this is to seek difficult challenges and work through the resistance to build grit. If we had an out for every time we came up against resistance, the human race would have perished by now. Resistance makes us stronger and more adaptable. If we never learn to adapt to the lessons of resistance, then we'll suck at life. Sometimes having our backs against the wall and having to push back is the only recourse to the resistance life offers us.

Life isn't free, and pursuing life isn't an entitlement; it's a choice and requires grit. We were bought with a price. I guess it was more like a sacrifice. The only thing we're entitled to is opportunity. Death is wrapped brightly and in very deceiving means on the path of least resistance. Life, bountiful and abundant, is found in resistance on the path to kingdom living.

SUFFERING

Yeah, I'm going to speak more about suffering, because I like it so much and it's important. My advice is to get real about it. Like pain, suffering is a part of life. But here's a neat point— suffering is a choice. Why not make the choice and set the boundaries about what to suffer for? If you want it bad enough, you'll be willing to hurt for it as you race death. This is a great way to show death you're not an easy mark. You aren't going to quit on life. Life doesn't owe us anything. Our parents, our employer, the weather ... they owe you nothing. Suffering is a choice, and a good one.

We can all define suffering and what it means and does for us. What we're willing to suffer for should cause no harm to others ... remember that. Along the way you may find a tribe with the same ideals as you, and they'll help you in your suffering.

Some people don't get to choose what they have to suffer. That's the part of life that isn't fair. Some people are more dignified in their suffering than others. I don't know why there's so much suffering in the world. I believe a great deal of it comes from how far we've drifted from our Creator. Mass shootings, terrorist attacks, domestic violence are things we hear about too frequently these days. People often question why God allows so much suffering. The answer is that He has no choice. God doesn't interfere in our choices and how we live. He's willing to help us and give us guidance, but He gives us the choice about living in relationship with Him. God offers us the wisdom and knowledge to reduce the impact suffering has on us. We need to leverage this as we pursue. We make the mistake of trying to rely on ourselves and on societal things, like governments and other entities. When we allow God to work within us, that changes how we suffer. It doesn't eliminate it, but it can change our perspective.

Suffering is important to study because of how real it is and what it can bring. It can bring learning if we're willing to check into that way of thinking. We need to step up into the place of an observer so we can see it in progress. We should aim to grow from our suffering. Suffering doesn't have to be a solitary experience. We can ask for assistance and leverage people who have walked the same path. Once we overcome the suffering and learned the lesson, we see how grit works in action.

Deliberate Practice

There's one magic bullet I do recommend to help you fully pursue life—work! I'm not going to try and minimize it or sugar-coat it. Hard work is the one thing that will always move you toward your objectives. If you're averse to hard work or hope that someone will come and do it for you, I wish you luck. Work smarter and create a system that helps you use your energy in a way that doesn't burn you out. Gritty, hard word is often the best option to make things happen.

I used to like the image of the Renaissance man. The idea of cultivating a persona or personal attitude as a Renaissance man appealed to me. Many people are capable of this mindset and skill, and for them it's a way of life. I now tend to think that maybe it's unrealistic in today's culture and may stretch us too thin. The image is cool, but I don't believe it's realistic (for me).

In my own experience and in what I've witnessed in others, deliberate practice, or the art of bringing into focus those things that matter most, accelerates our pursuit. When we cultivate deliberate practice, we create a laser-focus within ourselves and in our energy.

Deliberate practice brings us into a position of personal power … a power that emotionally connects to this art. We pursue it because we're passionate, deliberate in our choices, and desiring a specific outcome. We create a perfect storm within ourselves to give us power. We narrow our intention to a specific point of focus. Rather than energy dissipating in different directions, it slowly concentrates for maximum results. It is work, but it's your work of art.

DELIBERATE

Being deliberate about our actions means being conscious and intentional. As an athlete, I've been in the zone, a place where our energies all converge into intense yet relaxed effort. The mind and body fall into a relaxed trance from which the effort just flows. I can do this because I've forged deliberate practice into my life.

The study of scripture provides a good analogy for deliberate practice. The power and wisdom found in scripture allows us to be deliberate, as we can study daily and meditate on passages that will help us in our walk. There are two ways to go about doing this. We can sit with our Bible, phone at the ready, television on, and our day planner out to peruse. Our minds can be focused on all of the details of our day. Some of the scripture we partially pay attention to may take hold and even have a minor impact. Another approach is to be deliberate in our focus on scripture. We can seclude ourselves in a quiet place. Maybe we have a highlighter and a notebook so we can take notes about the message we receive from the passage. It's time spent in the moment with intention and purpose. We take our mind to a state of select concentration, with nothing to distract us from what we intend to accomplish. At this moment we have no other needs; we are being deliberate.

The mind is a powerful ally in your quest to pursue life. You have to win in the mind first. Deliberate practice aims at creating a mind of obedience. Ever question why your mind goes all over the place, or why you continually fall back into those old mental patterns? It's because your mind is obedient to societal conditioning. We are bombarded with information, images, and all manners of distraction to keep us slaves to the status quo.

Turn it all around and give your mind new information, images, and training to make it obedient to what you want to pursue. As a coincidence, we're asked to be obedient to God. Deliberate practice is the blueprint for any kind of obedience to your pursuit. Be openminded about obedience, because it's not a negative thing. It can actually be freeing. Biblical obedience is all about racing death on a spiritual level. By learning scripture and moving in it through life, we align with the promise of eternal life. How can that kind of obedience be bad? Eliminate the ego mindset, and life becomes a lot more open as limits are broken down. That is winning in the mind first.

Deliberate practice is an awesome grit builder. Grit is developed in the mind. It starts with mental energy and spreads to physical actions that become habits. Want to take control of your life and remove the old patterns and habits that are limiting you? Start building deliberate practice habits into all the areas you really desire to pursue.

PRACTICE

The application of our passion and intention isn't going to happen without practice. Theorize about it all you want, but it needs to be action in motion. Many theories exist about how many hours of practice it takes to become an expert. The 10,000-hour mark appears to be a common denominator. I don't know how many hours it would take for you to become the master of your art. I actually don't care. What I do know is that if you want it bad enough, you'll put in whatever time you need to do it.

One way that will help you become an expert in your own art is to live it. Don't sit around and expect someone else to live it for you—that's nuts. Deliberate practice means living each day in a way that expresses your Vision on some level. Let's not make practice out to be hard to do … it's easy. Seriously, if you have a Vision, it's easy to take some action daily toward it.

Practice can be boring and tedious. In today's "get it now" culture, practice is becoming a lost art. I've been blessed to cross paths with many individuals who model deliberate practice in their lives to the point of mastery. Across the board in their professions, their pursuit in training, in racing, and in all areas of their lives comes with practice. They also all understand the value of time and realize that time spent practicing is like compound interest on money. It works for you even when you're not fully able to see the results. Time is the great equalizer that moves us toward our Vision when we commit to practice. You can never practice too much. Your level of mastery depends on it. In life, your "why" has to be bigger than your "but."

DISTRACTION

Distraction is the enemy, and it thrives in full force all around us. We are inundated every moment by distraction. It's a billion-dollar industry which has become the norm in society. Handheld devices are the most distracting of all. We live online—gaming, streaming, texting, and not paying attention to the moment. It's the norm to have a cellular phone. A television and computer are standard equipment in homes. Our minds are targeted every second, and it's nearly impossible to avoid being distracted.

The distraction of the spirit is most concerning. We lose our inner guide with the constant bombardment of a world pulling us from ourselves to another place. We've become escape artists by not wanting to face what we are or live in the moment. Our ability to overcome obstacles is rooted in our ability to not become distracted. In order to master ourselves, we need to reverse the idea of tuning out (from ourselves) to tuning into (ourselves). Once we're that deeply aware of our own special and unique structure, we have no need to step outside of ourselves. Everything we require and need is designed in our very nature.

The cure for distraction rests in committing to and taking the time for deliberate practice. The mind is our ally and will support us in our practice as it follows the patterns and habits we set out for it. Turn the tables on distraction with simple ways to overcome them. Turn your phone off and make a pact with yourself to avoid it for ten minutes at a time. Then stretch that out into fifteen minutes and so on. We have the ability to release ourselves from the grip of distraction by creating measurable and achievable targets.

FOCUS ON WHAT YOU WANT

We often spend time and energy focusing on the things we don't want in our lives. We expend energy on eliminating unwanted habits and other things we dislike. Ironically, the more we focus on what we don't want, the more of it we get. It's an energy vortex that pulls us back into the same patterns and habits we're trying to eliminate. The focus is wrong, the energy is wrong, and we feel the weight of these issues as we try to change.

To turn things around, focus more on what you really want in life. Make your mind a steel trap that catches all the positive and necessary stuff you want. Maybe in a day you do two bad things and one good thing. Focus on the energy of that one good thing. Make that the light you see yourself through. Build it, nurture it, and create it so that there's no room for falsehood to weasel its way in.

Focus is the greatest mental ability and energy you can cultivate ... and you can cultivate it! It takes work but has unmeasurable value. Don't shy away from work—get gritty and dig in! Get beat up by the work. Get bloodied and battered, and then come back stronger and smarter. If you're not willing to do all of that, then quit right now! Yes, I said it ... quit right now. There will always be an excuse and a way out. The work is the only way through.

It's not just about positive thinking. Yes, there's great merit in positive thinking, but negative things happen. I can't control all of that, so I focus on what I can control. That's a positive lifestyle habit I work on integrating into my mental approach to life. I can choose how I react to anything negative. Focus more on the things you want in your life, and that energy is unstoppable.

PHILOSOPHY

Philosophy needs to be deliberately practiced. In our society it's easy to have your own philosophy beaten out of you. Societal conditioning can take the very philosophy you hold in your heart and make you deny or doubt it. If doubt sets in a smidge, you can be on a slippery slope.

Your philosophy is your basic personal operating system; it's what directs you toward your Vision. A sound philosophy that *you* create and live is essential to success. Societal conditioning tries to set a philosophy for you to live by. Create the philosophy that speaks to your true nature and stirs your heart. If you find yourself questioning something, good!

If it doesn't resonate in your heart, then it doesn't have a place in your life. You can respect the entity feeding you the philosophy, but you don't have to buy in.

The hard part is filtering out all the crap society feeds us. Too often we assimilate behaviour because it pleases others, even if it overrides our own needs. Never allow pleasing others to create an imbalance in life that leaves you void or broken. Serving others is different than trying to please them. Serving others is helping them and caring for them, whereas pleasing them is trying to make them like you.

Philosophy is either in control of you, or you're in control of your philosophy. Getting basic can help you find the essential building blocks of a personal philosophy. Start by decluttering your mind. Do an inventory of where your philosophy building blocks came from. What are the major influences that make up your personal operating system? This is a good exercise in discovering the path you're travelling and how your philosophy brought you here. Dig into yourself and get to the root. No judgement, no blaming anyone or anything. Just discover why you have the philosophy you do. What blocks do you want to keep? What blocks aren't in place that you want to have? How can you fully invest yourself in your pursuit by really nailing this philosophy down? It's an exercise that can bring inner clarity and mental peace. You're taking concrete steps in formulating a way to live that crazy, beautiful Vision. If it means taking a day, a month, or a year to get this straight, do it. This will help guide you all the way through racing death.

OBJECTIVES

In my coaching I've come to realize the power of how we word things. Some words carry negative connotations for some people but not for others. The word "goal" can carry a totally cuckoo/mental stigma for some. Read any literature on motivation and inevitably the word "goal" will come up. Realistically, we need goals to be successful. The clearer and more precise the goal, the easier it is to achieve. I get tired of the standard shape of fitness motivation and the motivation literature that's out there. Not all highly motivated or successful people follow the norms and standard practices that are prescribed in the mainstream motivation philosophy.

One of the most successful athletes I knew doesn't create elaborate goals. His success is based on actions that he deems necessary for his progress. He defines progress as his feeling of satisfaction and how much joy he experiences in the actions he uses. My friend simplifies things down to almost childlike plans, because he doesn't like to get caught up in the minutia and wasted time of excessive planning. This dude's business achievements and athletic accomplishments are off the charts. He races death hard and with intention, so that no matter what happens, he has the satisfaction of knowing he has done everything in his power to achieve it. He has his objectives, and he attacks the result they will bring. He uses the word "objective" over "goal," as it's "simpler," he says. His advice is to take one small action a day that brings you joy over ten that suck the life out of you but you think are productive.

After receiving this advice, I simplified all of my training plans and philosophy to take away any component that would be a distraction. It was hard at first, because I was used to doing things a certain way. Over time, though, I saw that the gains were worth all of the sacrifice. My objectives were clear, and that allowed my focus to become greater. With greater focus and less to attend to, I also found that my self-discipline became more attuned to what I was trying to accomplish. Creating manageable, measurable, and fun objectives was the key. The word "objective," for me, is nicer than the word "goal." My results were brought forth by the joy of a simpler way and practice.

TRANSFORM

Deliberate practice allows us to change the things we want to change in order to work toward our pursuit. We should continually transform, as that means we're growing. Growth means we're learning, and when we learn, we move. Moving is a true difference maker in our lives, and it can also be the difference in other people's lives. To not transform leads to decay; it leads to living in apathy and mediocrity. Those all help the status quo thrive and win. Believe me, this is a battle we're waging—a battle for your right to pursue life. This life is a gift and was bought at a great price. When we transform, we become a beacon to others and we lift them up in their own pursuit to overcome the status quo. We rise above the status quo.

It's positive and healthy to work to continuously transform. Remaining the same blocks our natural energy flow and we become dulled to the energy of the world around us. When we're locked in an energy block, we lose connection to our own place and purpose in life. We can release great energy through transformation and get so swept up in the energy of the positive that we don't have to work as hard to manifest positive emotions.

I was asked a cool question recently: "What would your life look like if you didn't have those voices inside locking you into these patterns?" Man! I will always tell you that I'm a work in progress. This question made me realize that I still have some old patterns I struggle to be rid of because of the voices I allow to hold me there. I've come a long way, but there's still work to be done. The thought of what life would look like without those voices is very enticing and looks really cool. I choose deliberate practice to free myself from limiting thoughts and ways that no longer serve me. There's a great freedom in a mind transformed and a body released from untruths.

Wonder

Let's take on the attitude of a child as we pursue life. Forget what you already know and what you think you know. Imagine that all you dream about is possible. Forget about the rules for once and choose to abandon fear. Take the clock off your wall and forget what time it is. Pursue life from the perspective of wonder.

Can you determine how many years you have left to live? Do you ever wonder about that? Seriously, have you ever had a conversation in your head about the amount of life you may have left to do what you want? Maybe this is something that you even worry about! These thoughts become a weight on your very being. Turn it around now with the power of wonder. We have to stop limiting ourselves with unrealistic measures and constraints. Fill up your mental sail with wonder and let it take you along where it may. The limits that occupy your mind are not always what they seem. In actuality, they may be seamless, invisible, and mostly untrue.

ABSOLUTES

We are creatures of habit. The thoughts and actions we exhibit become habit, and we decide to stay mired in those thoughts and actions. We set absolutes to keep ourselves in the safe zone, the zone we're familiar with and know so well. Security is a wide-scale societal pursuit. Is security important? Yes, it is. Is the security we have as sound and reliable as we're led to believe? Check out the status of the oil industry, the global economy, and the systematic terror cells that continually change the landscape. Nothing is absolute except for God's love.

Absolutes are necessary in many areas. We need moral and ethical absolutes to make living together as humans safer, peaceful, and possible. Absolutes create a modicum of normalcy, but when we hold to personal absolutes, we often believe things about ourselves that aren't absolute and true. Because of comfort levels, we make decisions not to do or even try different things. Then we convince ourselves that it's a lifelong absolute. We draw a line in the sand for ourselves. Absolute lines in the sand, closed minds, and the refusal to look at things from a different perspective all make pursuing life more difficult. This isn't how to step out into exciting, passion, driven life pursuit. We must aim to expand our minds beyond absolutes.

INNER CHILD

I think this is much easier for men than women, and I don't mean that in a bad way. Men never really grow up. We function, put on game faces, and honour our commitments. Underneath it all is a big kid. This inner child is an important ally when we choose to pursue our Vision. Children are naturally curious and accept uncontrolled and radical adventure better than adults. It's hard not to get caught up in adulating. You know, all that serious pie chart, mortgage, and appearances at dinner parties stuff adults are supposed to do. Blah ... I get that it's necessary, but it can also pull us down like an anchor.

Permission to let down the adult guard and be a kid is freely given. Playing is an important part of full on life pursuit. Play is a creative outlet and often leads to great strides in our personal capabilities. Our career life and parenting can lead to certain habitual mentalities and thought patterns. We flow in the same skills on a daily basis, which hypnotize us into that way of being. Enter your inner child. Let yourself go, whatever it takes, do it. Have a blast going out for a play date and not having to worry about adulating. Kids don't worry a lot; they just follow their energy and behave like kids.

Lack control sometimes and just be a kid. Explore that hobby you've always wanted to do but didn't because you were busy. Life is never out of reach for our inner child. The creativity, energy, and passion held inside will be released and start a new fire within you that will help you pursue from the perspective and innocence of a child.

NATURE

Is there any nature where you live? Find it, get into it, and explore it. A human connection gets turned on when we immerse ourselves in nature. We connect, feel, and experience a close connection with creation. Balance and value come from the peace we receive in a natural setting. When we immerse ourselves in places where nature is prevalent, we release positive energy trapped within by concrete, noise, lack of space, and getting caught up in it all. Nature can heal the mind, which in turn creates a different inner landscape. This inner landscape revitalizes our overall health. This is a good way to reset our physical body by letting go. Nature offers us a quiet, which lowers stress levels and decreases the attack on our sensory perceptions. This is a huge daily attack we just ignore because it's become the norm in society. Guard your personal energy. Find quiet, peaceful ways to recharge and repair the damage.

Nature offers us a learning environment. We can learn that we're not as important or significant as we believe we are. When we see how we make all our problems more important than they really are, we free ourselves from their power. In nature we see life and death, renewal and decay. Nature never lies; nature is our creator in our midst. When in nature, all the conditioning can be stripped away. We can see the world as God intended it. We see a true reflection of ourselves. We are human; nature offers us the chance to be human without asking for anything in return.

If the feeling of peace escapes you, I suggest getting out into nature. The feeling of pressure easing off our souls is so beneficial. Nature is a drug that alters our entire physical reaction to the world. We are a sensory machine cut off from our source in cities and disconnected from source energy. Our grid is not energized cement and the noise it holds. Our grid recharges in nature and we become balanced as an organism.

It's difficult when you're out in nature not to feel a sense of wonder at the majesty and immenseness of it all.

CHALLENGE

Looking to step out of the mundane existence of the status quo into the incredible world of wonder? One word will help you: challenge. Here's a new concept for you to step into: Challenge everything you believe. Challenge everything you hear. Challenge all conversations in your head. Challenge life; challenge death.

What makes an expert an expert? Education and popular opinion? I don't know. I'm an expert in my field at work, but I can sure as heck be wrong. Being an expert doesn't equate to perfection. To be challenged in your expertise is a good thing. Be open to it and willing to expand in wonder of the possibilities it can create.

We lose our sense of wonder when we get locked onto and into our belief systems. God didn't say close your mind and believe only for the sake of believing. God wants us to open our minds to the immense possibility of His creation and love for us. When our minds are closed in our beliefs, we can even have a closed mind to what is powerful about the truth in those beliefs. We should challenge ourselves daily with questions about our direction. We can challenge the status quo, our own actions, the actions of others, and God. Wow, did you just say challenge God? Yes, I did, and yes, I do. God allows us to challenge Him and what He's bringing into our lives. We can't just argue for the sake of argument and wanting to have our own way. That's not how challenging God works. God allows us to challenge Him in prayer, in our conversations with Him. God loves that and wants us to step up into that aspect of the relationship. To challenge God on things is to want to learn and grow for the sake of the Vision He has provided for you.

We are challenging the way of the world when we radically choose to overcome the status quo. You become a rebel when you think or act in a way that takes apart the societal conditioning that holds the fabric together in mediocrity. We must challenge the mentality that allows for only one way of doing or looking at things. When the system isn't working for all the people, there's a problem. Sometimes we have to understand that we're a part of the bigger picture, and we need to relinquish certain things for the good of all. The sense of wonder to believe that there's a better way, or that we can do more for others, can change the world. Acting unselfishly to create a better world really is an amazing way to challenge the status quo. Connecting with God will help you find your Vision, and He'll bring you to the challenges that will help you live that Vision. Man, it's a cool life when we're moving in that Vision and living in alignment with God.

THE THEORY OF POSSIBILITY

This mathematical theory deals with certain types of uncertainty and has something to do with the Theory of Probability. Math was not my forte, and I really admire people with a mind that can wrap around all those rules and things. My theory of possibility goes something like this: nothing is possible if possibility is not an option. Seems like a pretty easy theory to understand. Unfortunately, I've observed far too often people who see no possibility of creating what they envision, and the whole media machine really feeds this mindset. It takes less energy to remain negative and down than it does to create change. Change is the elusive mystery that people want but don't know how to create. Lacking the ability to see what's possible is the biggest roadblock.

Possibility can be the great equalizer; the smallest glimpse of possibility can spark the greatest uprising in your life. Possibility is a form of hope for something better. I want a lot of things that are just out of my reach right now, but the possibility of achieving them uplifts me and encourages me to continue moving my energy properly to achieve them. This book was originally just an idea. It became a possibility when I sat down and wrote the first words. The possibility you might buy it and read it moved my energy to complete it.

The most powerful part of my theory is that you and I can control the outcome. It's always possible to respond to your circumstance from a place of higher awareness as opposed to from a lower level energy. The more cognizant you become of your ability to bring about a better possibility in all areas of your life, the more you'll see those possibilities become reality. When we start to work in the theory of possibility, we change the shape of energy.

The possibilities for you are endless—but be aware that possibility works in both directions. Be negative and you'll possibly attract more negativity into your life. Abundance in all the things you want is waiting when you turn the energy upside down and hit the theory of possibility full on. The smallest shift in focus can start the process and begin to bring about better results. Take a simple step each day to focus on possibilities, and the possibility that tomorrow will be better is highly likely.

MAVERICKING

Not even sure that "mavericking" is a word, and I don't care. I'm using it. I'm a proponent of going against the tide of unethical ways we're subjected to on many levels in society. We don't have to be passive wimps in life because of fear. Being a non-conformist in your world can help others free themselves from this mentality. Standing against injustice will always feel better than being in the herd and secure. Man, I can't tell you how many times I should have spoken up but didn't. I should have raised my voice and at least rocked the boat enough to be heard. Some things haunt me because I didn't have the guts to man up.

I'm not against inclusive, healthy thinking, especially when it comes to the treatment of others. Discrimination is wrong. Racism is wrong. Hatred is wrong, whether it's against a woman, homosexual, non-Caucasian, or any religious group or minority. All life matters; all humans are created equal, and God loves each and every one of them. Political correctness is not the way to change radical behaviour or an unfair culture. It's just a stop-gap measure that creates more tension amongst groups. I'm not an expert in this area, so my comments will be limited to that extent.

If you're a maverick and your mavericking harms no one, then maverick on! Mavericks alter and change the shape of the status quo. We need more mavericks in the world, people willing to pursue the truth and attack death to create more life. A maverick doesn't have to be confrontational or rude. A maverick just has the conviction to confront the status quo and alter the way of mediocrity. A maverick works in ways that harms no others, he or she is always willing to work in accord with people and to listen and be open to new ways of doing things. Mavericks wonder about all the possibilities their energy can create and the holes they can punch in the universe. To maverick and make a difference changes the world and alters the status quo.

IGNITE

A life not on fire is a life filled with unfulfilled dreams. Ignite the power of a person so filled with wonder for your own potential that you can surf on the tidal wave of energy you create. Who cares if it seems unrealistic? Don't judge the fire ... feed it and see where it takes you. When we live with an extinguished spirit, every little thing becomes an obstacle, a limiting belief or boundary. When we ignite our entire being by opening up to a new challenge or opportunity, we tip the balance. We are our own worst enemies at times in our pursuit. We start to reason away whether it's the right time. We use logic to talk ourselves out of the possibility of failure. All our fired-up energy is consumed in false fears and societal ways that teach us to not rock the boat, and we die millions of small deaths in our lifetime. We need to stop listening to the lies. Ours is a life filled with nothing but extreme potential to change the shape of our own energy.

Building a front and centre Vision in our minds allows us to ignite our passion. It's not always easy, but it's possible. As we learn to ignite our fire and it grows, we start to control what we really want trending in our lives. Our art becomes the reality we see ourselves from, and we grow our brand. OUR BRAND is a flowing river that no one can alter or contain. It comes from a healthy place within and becomes the outer expression of our true nature, our brand. This is how I define living remarkable. To live remarkable is to ignite the power of your true nature so that nature fuels a revolution in our world—a revolution of art and spirit-freeing energy so unique it punches a hole in the universe. Igniting our pursuit to see way beyond our cheating, false beliefs opens our entire being to the real potential of life. Racing death is going to push us out beyond the entire depth of our experiences. Life ignited by the cross extinguishes death.

Narrative

We spend a lot of time in our own minds, which is natural because it's a safe place to have conversations and roll ideas around. When it comes to pursuing our Vision and stepping into pursuit of life, our narrative will either make or break our success. How we manage our thoughts, internal dialogues, and the inner landscape of the mind is essential to living. Ours is a mind to use for powerful pursuit and connection to Vision. Inside our minds lies a vast quantity of ability to create or to destroy. All of the ideas, thoughts, imaginings, and words we roll around in our mind will determine how we live this journey.

Have you ever had a false perception of what you're really capable of? I think we all have a time we can look back on when we sold ourselves short because of a false narrative we were holding in our mind. Fear is a major player upstairs and in holding us back. Fear-driven narratives wreak havoc on our pursuit if we don't see through the smoke and veil keeping us from moving into the truth. It takes very little energy for these false perceptions to start and begin rolling downhill on us. It takes a lot more energy to overcome the false perceptions and start to move. The energy expenditure is worth every ounce once you learn to control your narratives.

"Control" is a key word, and control starts with monitoring what you're thinking. Top performers have far fewer thoughts in a day, because they've learned to control what they focus on. Top performers work tirelessly to keep the mindless drivel of poor narrative out of their own heads. Quality thinking is something we can grow in our minds so that it takes hold in all areas of our lives.

THE LOOP

Our internal chatter and conversations may become a loop we hear over and over. In our minds we have the ability to create unaltered conversations. These unaltered conversations are safe because we don't have to share them with others. They're ours; they allow us an outlet or a creative force. This loop can also become a self-destructive force that drains our energy. We can create internal beliefs that we prefer over the realities we're actually living. We build arguments, slights, perceived injustices, and other negative emotional states. We start to live in our minds, and those inner thoughts become our realities.

Around and around this internal chatter goes, and soon we're not even aware that we're having these internal conversations. The voices and negative force multipliers take over. Force multipliers are tools that help you amplify your own effort to produce more output. They should be positive tools, and when used well they really are amazing; however, your mental loop can become negative force multipliers that overrun all other thoughts.

Overriding the loop and creating a new one is worth taking time to work on. Start replacing these old loop thoughts with small changes in your self-talk. Creating simple, small affirmations you can repeat over and over that require little time is easy: "I'm mentally strong." "I'm mentally quiet." "I believe in myself." Say them ritually so that they become the inner reality you can move into your outer world. We live what we say in our heads. Changing the inner landscape helps us change or create the outer landscape we desire. Once you begin to control the loop rather than allowing it to control your life, life moves in different currents. The energy we're able to bring to our pursuit is greatly impacted for the better.

THE WITNESS (SPIRIT)

Step out of your mind and into your heart. Having a sensor to help us with our narrative is as simple as tuning into your heart. Your witness is quietly waiting for you to defer the wild order of your mind to the power of the Spirit. Your Vision is based on passion, a statement of you as a person and what you're willing to pursue. It's an emotional band, and you have to tune into what's important to you in life. In that band is your spirit. If we lose our perspective, or our reality becomes distorted, this is the place we want to turn for guidance and to find our calm.

Truth is sometimes relative and sometimes absolute. Left to the mind, we usually defer to a relative perception, which places us as the judge of what is true. Many problems arise from this due to a skewed perception. Not to say our perceptions are all bad or wrong, but we don't normally like to be wrong. It's natural to manipulate our perceptions to suit our needs and wants. In order to be more accurate and more productive in pursuing our Vision, we need help. The spirit is objective, honest, and willing to push us toward the real truth. The spirit will not dictate because it always gives us a choice. That's the beauty of the witness we have in our spirit. It's compassionate and filled with empathy. The mind can lean toward being a bully when it wants to be right.

Things can get stormy and volatile within the mind. Ideas, opinions, and arguments can become a normal, daily wave of activity. It can get so busy we lose energy, focus, and our ability to control the demons that rise up. All of this stuff can hamper the quality of our pursuit path and harm our Vision. Once out of control, this sends us careening out of our true orbit to a place in the universe we don't want to be. Our mind simply overruns us and we feel lost, vulnerable to what we perceive as attacks, and ultimately disabled in our abilities.

The spirit brings perspective from a higher place within you. The heart has a balancing effect that we can use to gauge the truth of our narrative. We work in tandem with the spirit as a partnership. The Vision we pursue had its roots in the spirit, and we align our energy when we take our narrative to the spirit level. Having this witness allows us to truly be aware of the way we speak in our own minds. Taking the mind to task is essential to our success. We're not to be slaves to our minds; it is a tool we should control. Live with a relationship based on the spirit monitoring your narrative to gain the upper hand and move to the place of being in control of that narrative.

OTHERS' VOICES

Can you hear the voices in your life that were well meaning but squashed your Vision? They wanted what was best for you without understanding what was best for you. Their fears were speaking, and they may have caused you to halt your pursuit of life the way you were designed to pursue it. You may need to forgive people who have hurt you with their fears. Don't harbour anger, as that will keep you from releasing your greatness into the world.

Examine all the voices and influences in your life. We are inundated daily with information from peers, advertising, family, and untold numbers of sources attacking our minds with narratives. The narratives used to manipulate you to capitulate are clever, and some are very dark. As we grow up, we become accustomed to the manipulative narratives because we think they're normal. These narratives are disguised as free speech and our "rights." The control mechanisms supposed to protect us are antiquated and in it for themselves. You are the keeper of the narrative that will propel you past the junk. Your narrative is not for sale and should never be open to manipulation.

Draw a line in the sand here. Take control of this inner dialogue and your own story. Be open-openminded. An open mind can be a strong and discerning mind. It's a free mind that will build a narrative that is informed and powerful enough to do what is right and ethical. Self-talk is a massive component of our narrative, and the greatest of care needs to be taken in this area. I used to joke about being slow and hating training. I thought it was innocent enough and funny; however, over time I started to notice the impact this kind of joking self-talk had on my mind and my fitness. Be careful what you tell yourself about your lifestyle. No one can harm you more than your own words. Guard what you say in your own mind and don't allow the unhealthy narrative to live there.

FORGET EVERYTHING YOU THINK YOU KNOW

Have you ever been at that point in an argument where you can't remember what your argument really is? You're working on a point, and in the back of your mind you're trying to find what it was all about!

People argue to be right even if it's not really important. Being right at all costs is more important than debating a point and trying to see the opposite point of view. Allow yourself to be wrong every now and again … it's liberating!

I learned some valuable lessons about forgetting what I think I know from training, racing, and failing. In many ways in training I'm a creature of habit. If it ain't broke, don't fix it. Unfortunately, that can often lead to being more broken than progressive. I have my staple workouts that will always be part of my regimen. Changing up the way and the why of those workouts is important to progressing and keeping it fresh. Boring can set in fast and rip the fun out of training. Allowing for new information to be explored helps keep the mind open and growing. Exploring new information opens new pathways to growth through learning about better ways to train. Exploring new pathways keeps the spirit enervated and makes pursuit exciting—and it should be exciting.

The age factor plays a part in forgetting everything you think you know. At fifty-four, I have to change things up. In many ways I'm stronger in some aspects than I used to be, but there are areas that require more attention than when I was younger. I have to focus differently on eating and recovery; however, I find more joy in why I do all of this, as it's no longer just about results, swag, and medals. The path God chose for me continues to unfold through all of this training and competing. I still have to stop myself from falling into the "know-it-all" mindset, but God is infinitely patient.

It's a fun experiment to take stock of your "know-it-all" places. Maybe at work you can free up energy to take on new challenges and open new doors. Are there places in your relationships that are keeping you stuck because of stale and old knowledge? Move to a place of genuine excitement for new knowledge and ideas in your relationships. Is your religion keeping you from the truth of God? Dogma is a great suppressor of the light that can really shine in your life from God's wisdom and knowledge. Forget all the stored-up untruths about yourself. Open the mind to the infinite possibilities you're capable of exploring. The power of pursuit is going to create a new level of knowledge from which you can see life.

FACE YOUR INSECURITIES

This opens up an uncomfortable door. I have insecurities … yup, it's true. They lurk behind my built-up strength and false fronts. These insecurities can be in narratives waiting to pounce and pull me into the old mindset of a powerless abuse victim. That's where my insecurities take me, because they're grounded in the aftermath of the energy the abuse created. No, I'm not looking for sympathy; it's not needed. This is just a simple truth. I've built a new mindset that moves me to a higher love for myself and an energy that overrides the past. Having said that, I still battle with insecurities.

In order to create a better narrative than the one born from my insecurities, I needed to name my insecurities. How do you name your insecurities? I discovered that you just need to be honest about them with yourself. That level of honesty helped me name them and then move into a new personal power to deal with them. Giving these insecurities an identity helped me create better narratives that moved me into a different relationship with the insecurity. I can't say that I'll ever fully be over the insecurities, but I'm much more capable of dealing with them when they rise up. This is where the true ability to change the insecurity comes from. This isn't just positive self-talk. Creating a narrative about yourself to help defeat insecurity helps raise the truth about yourself over the untruth of the insecurity. The feeling moves from a place of fear and uncertainty to a place of power and certainty.

Being a man, I'm supposed to be strong and not cry, right? Well, here's the truth … I cry, I can be weak, and that's something that has helped me on the path of creating a good internal narrative. To not have weakness is unrealistic. I know what things cause me to feel weak and insecure, so why fight it unrealistically with super macho male bravado? If I don't acknowledge my insecurities, they just lie beneath the surface and have power over me. I'll never gain control over them. I have the ability to move up to a place of truth within myself and create a new way to accept that I am not perfect and that my insecurities are there. The insecurities aren't real, and the narrative I create and run in my mind is what will move me over the top and into the position of control.

I encourage you to seek help in overcoming your insecurities. Talk with a professional to gain a different perspective and acquire tools to assist you. We're all different, and that's beautiful. Insecurities will affect you differently than they affect me. I've worked with professionals to create a different narrative and perspective that has helped me greatly in moving beyond the energy of immobility to mobility regarding my insecurities. I believe in you and your ability to change the energy in your life and rise up into your true nature.

THE IMPOSTER

We all have an imposter residing within us. Maybe this character was a necessity in our life at some point in time. Perhaps we felt we needed to be this character in order to survive. Maybe this character helped us cope in life and to be a contributing member of society while we were in need of help. I know from personal experience that I had a character like this when I was young and dealing with being abused. It eventually became the strongest voice inside of me, and I started to live this imposter persona in all areas of my life. It became the voice of reason; it provided the necessary advice and guidance to allow me to survive; however, it was the furthest truth from my true nature. This imposter was not the real me; I was battling to get back to my roots. That was my own personal radical pursuit.

Societal conditioning had a part in the creation of this imposter. I had to create this imposter in my mind to protect others from the abuser who had used me as a boy. It's difficult to explain something like this, but here it is in a nutshell. When my abuser took liberties with me, he'd say, "Remember, these will be our little secrets." Because he was an authority figure and a blood relative (uncle), those words had immense power over young me. The day came when I realized that I had the power to stop it, and I did. Here is a twist that also may be hard to explain. When I was old enough to overcome the power of the "our little secret" hold on me and to truly hate the man who hid behind his priestly garb, I made another decision. What would the knowledge that their son was a pedophile and abused boys do to my grandparents? I made a decision I regret but can't change now. I remained silent. Judge me all you want for that decision... I'm cool with it. That decision created an imposter inside of me that I lived with until I was in my early thirties. Trying to undo that way of living took another ten years and massive emotional, mental, and spiritual battles. Even now talking about this is difficult for me, because my mom is still alive. I don't want her to have to hear this, which is why I don't expound much on the abuse. It happened; I have created a platform to hopefully protect others from it.

The imposter isn't really going to do what we need or require. It's a false voice that keeps us in line or takes us in the direction of societal conditioning. I created an imposter within to face the wicked truth of being a sexual abuse survivor, and the wicked truth about a lack of justice. But to remain in that imposter mindset was not going to free me. I worked to change the way I walked my walk, because God showed me a better way, a truth that would set me free. As we're told in Romans 2:12, we can be transformed by Him working within us. We don't have to be conformed to the ways of this world. I sought the wisdom and knowledge of the scriptures, and the imposter no longer had a place in my life. Overcoming this false narrative is possible because we have the greatest means available to do so. When we walk with the Spirit in our hearts and a mind transformed by our Creator, all of the false stuff falls away and a new way shines through.

OPINIONS

You're entitled to your opinion, even if it's wrong. Opinions are dangerous sometimes. Where do we get them from? Are they accurate? I heard an interesting perspective on why people argue. The theory was that people argue to be right. When people debate, they're willing to listen to another person's point of view and discuss it. When they argue, they want to be right. I like the way that's laid out. It's not about pushing your opinion on others or about having to be right. I think the world would be a better place if we were all willing to debate a little more and argue less.

Sometimes when we have opinions we close our minds to possibilities. Instead of trying to see new or better ways, we think that our ways are the right way. Being blind to a world of change and different opinions is dangerous. The mindset becomes stifling and creates realities that can be untrue and unhealthy. We need to ask ourselves if being right is more important than learning new ways to pursue, because an open mind is a way to discover and build new pathways and move the needle.

Having opinions isn't the issue, but if they become our default truths in the face of a changing world, we become unwilling to see that world for what it is. I don't always like the world I see, but if I create an opinion that insulates me from the truth, what have I accomplished? I've only fooled and limited myself. Greatness as we define it isn't something found in a static approach to living but in exploring the edges and where we sometimes don't feel like going. We need to move out of the opinionated places where we allow mental energy to die.

You and I are different, but we're alike as well. Somewhere in our collective intelligence we have much more in common than we think. Maybe that's the key right there. We need to think more about what each other is about than what's an absolute right in our own minds. The energy that created us is the same and runs through every one of our thoughts. When we decide to listen and try to understand what the other person is saying, we have more common ground. We don't have to agree on everything and change our opinions to appease the other person or for the sake of political correctness, but being a little more tolerant isn't a bad thing, and it can reduce stress and increase happiness and joy.

RADICAL ENTRY 10

The Seeker

I went through a strange process as I wrote this book. I had the racing death and radical pursuit concepts worked out before I even knew I was going to write it. I knew that the whole premise would surround how we received life when Jesus died for us on the cross. That's why we are to radically pursue life by every means laid out for us in scripture. Now we must be willing to find in the Word our daily bread, which includes our actions, thoughts, beliefs, values, mindset, voice, and our life template.

As I was writing, though, there was something missing ... something for me to learn and understand about myself that would move this work to a different place. During an incredible one-month period in November and December of 2016, I came to realize what and how I was missing. I was working within my timeline and control. The Lord helped me to grasp and understand His timeline for this project. God showed me the reason for this project while continuing to get the message out through my first book.

I was hanging out in Canmore, Alberta. God takes me here often for lessons in listening, trusting, and believing. I'd been feeling the pull for some time and settled on the weekend of December 17–18, 2016. The beauty and majestic awe of the place nestled in the Canadian Rockies is prime learning ground for me.

This is what God showed me as we hung out together: "Do not seek what you have already found." I sit here in Canmore and am now bolstered with great energy at what God taught me here." God told me not to seek what I have already found—Him! In my wanderings, I've continued to seek God in places, situations, and life experiences, rather than walking in His full presence and living His kingdom way. I was still seeking Him. I had given my heart to Christ fully in 2006. God said to me, "You need to live without fear of me not being here."

There's a gap between two mountains in Canmore. Ha Ling is to the east, and Rundle to the west. A road leads up from Canmore Nordic Centre and goes through this gap to take one into the back country. I've hiked up Ha Ling and the east side of Rundle. There are amazing views from up there, and the road between leads to a playground of hiking, mountain biking, rock climbing, and much more. In my Vision from God, I was looking south toward this gap. God was asking me to step through the gap into the wilderness. The physical spot between Ha Ling and Rundle was a metaphor, of course. God was teaching me that I needed to seek a different way, a different perspective, and to know I had already found His path for me. Now I was seeking something designed to move me away from my old limiting beliefs about myself.

SEEK WILDERNESS

The wilderness mindset is the opposite of the comfort zone. We tend to find pockets of comfort that are predictable. Even if we aren't happy, we live in these zones. God asks us to step into venues for exploring our true nature. The wilderness mindset frees us to be wild in a controlled way. Our minds become locked into reason and logic, so much so that those become the sole focal point of our mental faculties. We start to become like the tame wild animals in a zoo—apathetic and lethargic, even with all that true nature lying below the surface. We often are caged in our minds, where the societal conditioning has taught us that this is the only way to be. Life can become a cage.

Societal conditioning seeks to remove a wilderness mindset rather than promote a seeking mindset. It's not civilized to think in ways that don't align with the status quo. If you eliminate that kind of thinking, you eliminate opposition to your philosophy. It's how many of our cultural mainstays keep the status quo. Government as it is consumed by party ideology. Religion as it is consumed with creating disciples. The law as it is consumed with keeping the peace. I understand the need for social interdependence and upholding the values and morals of a society, but it goes too far when it's a means to remove opposition or exert control over people's minds.

Allowing our minds to embrace a wilderness mentality opens new ways to think and act. The steady-state thinking of habits and patterns often creates a rut. The world stops seeming to be exquisite and worth exploring and instead becomes a state of living dead. Life is an adventure to be explored; no daily task is done with mediocrity. We are living in each moment from a higher perspective. Our time is a measure in quality as opposed to something we need to kill. What a horrible expression: "Just killing time." In our wilderness thinking, time is life; it is precious and held in our hearts and minds as a valuable treasure. From the wilderness of your mind comes possibilities that are boundless, pursued with exuberance.

GOING MEDIEVAL, DARK

Sometimes I am civilized, in the societal way. The path presented offered easy and mainstream life. It looked healthy, but selling your soul for the wrong path is not truly living. I became focused on a purpose, a path, a state of life that wasn't in my own best interests. I bought the societal conditioning and tried to live on that path. Worst decision I ever made. I became mostly like a neutered man, not my own. Not in pursuit, but living dead.

Pursue life with vigour as long as we aren't harming others. But what if life is harming us? When we give away our power to societal conditioning as opposed to our true nature, life can take advantage of us. We believe it's right to watch people not perform properly, to break rules or laws because they feel that those laws don't apply to them. Bullies in white collar jobs who take advantage of their positions at the expense of others. We see it at every level of government and business; we can find corruption everywhere we look. And we have become blinded and conditioned by it all.

I believe in going medieval when life starts to create pain and hurt. Mentally I feel much better when I go out and suffer on a run, a bike, or some other tough workout. I take my energy and disgust for societal mediocrity and put it to work, making myself feel better and working to change things. This is all about becoming more resilient and fighting through the societal bureaucracy of life. Allowing my mind to break free from what is expected is going medieval. Not being predictable in all areas of life opens a medieval option to living. Medieval thinking is survival thinking and triggers mechanisms in our mind that get us to move. Thinking in different ways frees us from the herd mentality.

Exercise became way too pretty for a while. In some ways, it's still too pretty in a lot of circles. Fancy machines, fancy clothing, fancy shoes, and fancy plans became the norm. Exercise became less about being effective and more about an image. I like where a lot of street-style or other less pretty fitness philosophies are headed. Lower cost, more effective, and pushing the boundaries, these fitness movements have changed the landscape. I love how age has become a lesser measuring stick in fitness. People are getting after it no matter what age! One unusual side effect of the more medieval forms of training I've noticed is how much more encouraging and group stimulating these movements are. People are competing and pushing hard; however, there's less "me against you" and more "I'm here, you're here, we're going to push ourselves to the best possible versions of us we can be." It's very stimulating and encouraging to see the group dynamic these movements have created.

Going medieval borders on desperation for me. It's the place where my back is up against the wall and I need to fight and claw my way out of there. It's fun to go to a place where we want to push the envelope. Being safe and not hurting others always needs to be our top priority. Going medieval is playing with only seventeen marbles in your deck. Doing an Ironman or Ultramarathon means being a little off centre; it puts a person into a different level of mental. There's a medieval depth to pushing your body past the comfort zone to compete in these events and complete them. The real chase begins when we get medieval and it lights up our pursuit.

DO SOMETHING ABOUT IT

See that black cloud following you around? That's your attitude, your "go and get it" factor. That's the pity party hangover because it didn't go your way, and it has a lot to do with the definition of insanity—doing the same thing over and over but expecting different results. The seeker is continuously looking to improve, to innovate, and to grow personally. The only expectation the seeker has of life is what they create and how they pursue life. Yes, they have bad days and they get upset; seekers are human. The seeker doesn't sit in their own poopy pants and feel sorry for themselves. The seeker takes action and does something about it.

In my workplace, I observe many employees who feel their employer is responsible to make them happy. These people believe that the employer is responsible for their health and their prosperity. These employees don't play by the compound effect either. They abuse sick time, fail to provide any measure of good customer service, and are unreliable and needy. The level of drama that some of these employees bring daily to the workplace is childish and ridiculous. I'll support and have empathy for you on all levels; however, if you're not willing to act on your own behalf to change all that you hate or complain about, then don't blame your employer. The cost to the taxpayer because of this rampant attitude in the workplace is not acceptable.

The warriors I hang out with aren't needy and don't hold anyone responsible for their own well-being. These people are continually seeking new ways to live radical in their pursuit. Each day is an opportunity for them to move the needle to create the lifestyle to support their Vision. It's truly amazing to see the difference between these two kinds of individuals. The warriors I know who go medieval have one big difference from the people who want others to make their lives better—they hold themselves accountable. They understand that life is a gift, and they open it every day no matter what their circumstances. The warrior's mindset is to pursue life and kill death with every breath.

Moving to pursue life takes some moxie and a grit-based attitude. Making things happen takes trust and a belief in your ability to do what you want and what is required to achieve that Vision. Do something about all those things you can control, and don't focus on what you can't. Attack the places you know will open the crack in the darkness and explode into the light.

PURSUING LIFE IN IRELAND

I asked my Daughter Aislinn to write a chapter for this book. Here is what she provided:

The year 2017 has been pretty interesting so far. At the beginning of February, I quit a job I'd been at for about a year and a half. It wasn't an easy decision to make; however, it was time. Not having any plan as to what I'd be doing afterwards, I gave my boss one month's notice.

Shortly after handing in my notice, I booked a three-week trip to Ireland, by myself. A solo-backpacking trip is something I've always wanted to do, and the thought of looking for a new job right away was simply unappealing. I put a lot of thought into it. I went back and forth with the idea. Where would I go? Could I really do it alone? How long would I go for? No, I won't go … Okay, yeah, I'll go. I was scared. Even just the idea of going on a trip alone scared me. And that's when I realized that the fear I was feeling was the exact reason why *I had* to do it. So I started looking at flights, and the first place that came to mind was Ireland.

In September of 2015, my cousin, Erin, and I went backpacking together for five weeks. We spent one week in London, three and a half weeks in Ireland, and a few days in Iceland on our way back to Canada. Ireland is familiar to me. While looking at flights, I figured that I knew Ireland and how to get there. I missed it; I missed the green, not to mention the Guinness! I also have roots there. My great grandparents on my dad's side are from Northern Ireland, and a close family friend lives there as well. I call her my Irish Mom. It made sense, right? So I did it. On February 7, I booked my trip. I would leave on March 8. There was no going back.

The rest of February went by quickly. I don't think I actually processed anything until my last day of work. All of a sudden, I was leaving in one week and I had nothing planned or prepared. Even still, I left everything to the last minute. Suddenly it was the night before I was to leave, and I was having a full-blown melt down. *What have I done? Do I really have to go? Three weeks by myself … that's a long time. I can't do it.* So much self-doubt and fear-based thoughts consumed my mind as I packed what I needed, and I didn't need much. I lay in bed that night just hoping I'd get even a few minutes of sleep.

My dad woke me up the next morning with coffee. Thank goodness, or I may not have gotten out of bed. Then something shifted. I packed my stuff, gathered any last-minute items, and off I went. The panic had subsided and instead of fearful tears, I had happy tears. It hit me—the realization that I was doing this! Me! I was so proud of myself. This was something I'd always just talked about doing, and now suddenly it was happening.

My mom dropped me off at the airport. I remember looking back for her as I was standing in line at security. There was comfort in knowing she was close, but as soon as I passed through those metal detectors, I was on my own. Day one of twenty-one and I had three flights and fifteen hours of travelling ahead of me, but I was doing it.

It was surprisingly easy. I don't know why I was so scared in the first place. The flights went by fairly quickly, considering I had three of them. I landed in Dublin, hopped on a bus, and made my way to my hostel. I remember the freedom I felt walking through Dublin with just my backpack. I had three weeks, no set plans, and no one to worry about. It was just me, my backpack, and Ireland. I couldn't help but smile.

The following three weeks were some of the best days of my life to date. I met so many incredible people, all on their own journeys, pursuing life in their own way. I saw so many beautiful sights, not to mention I learnt so much about myself and how I want to pursue my own life. Self-discovery—they don't teach that in school. I often found myself asking the same question: Why hadn't I done this sooner? The answer was simple: I let my fear overpower my desire to live, my desire to experience life. I was scared of how my decisions would affect those around me (quitting my job). What would people think? I had no plan for when I got home. I'd be broke and jobless, but I'd figure it out when the time came.

If there's anything I've learnt about life, it's that life is just a series of highs and lows, routine and sudden change. All you can do is adjust accordingly. Not everything is in your control, and that's alright. However, some things are. If you feel like a chapter in your life is coming to a close, if something isn't serving you or making you happy anymore … surprise! You're allowed to move on!

Too often in life I've made decisions based on how they will affect others. The only problem with that is when I put others first, I'm ultimately putting myself last. It's not rude or selfish to put yourself first! Repeat that last sentence over and over to yourself until it sticks. Your happiness and sanity are *top* priority, no matter what anyone says. I'm not saying to go through life with absolutely no regard for how other people feel, or how your decisions affect those around you. Always do things with grace and respect but be unapologetic in your pursuit of life. You owe it to yourself.

On my trip I'd planned to bus around Ireland and re-visit some of the places I'd been before. I started in Dublin and from there I went to see my Irish mom and family in Northern Ireland. I spent three days in County Armagh being absolutely spoiled by Rosemary, Eamon, and their two girls. Irish hospitality is next level; I'll never be able to thank them enough for all they've done for me. The McNeils are truly exceptional human beings who fill my heart with so much love. From there I made my way to Galway. The night before I left the McNeils, that familiar feeling of panic set in—similar to what I felt the night before I set off on this journey. I had another meltdown; however, this time it was a little different. I acknowledged what I was feeling, but then I asked myself why I was feeling this way. The answer was simple: I was now leaving the comfort I'd found with the McNeils and shaking things up to move on into the unknown. I was once again going to be on my own; my fear was consuming my mind.

The next day they drove me to the bus station and off I went. I remember how stressed out I felt, until I put my headphones in and admired the rolling green hills as we drove through Ireland. I did a lot of reflecting on that bus ride. I remember taking a step back and asking myself why I was so stressed. Do I have any real reason to be stressed out here? If yes, can I do anything about it right this moment? If no, why am I stressed out in the first place? If I can do something about my stress, then I shouldn't be stressed at all! If I can't, I'll deal with it when the time comes, which again means I shouldn't even be stressed in the first place. Stress is pointless, and I've wasted so many nights stressing over things that are out of my control. Believe me when I say your energy could be put to better use.

I arrived in Galway and immediately fell back in love with the city. I had two nights booked there and then I'd be heading off to Killarney. Those two days were so perfect that when I got to Killarney, I decided two days in Galway wasn't enough. The next day I went back and ended up staying for two weeks. Part of me felt guilty for not moving around Ireland more with the time I had (again, worried about what people would think), but I found my place and I was happy to stay. Those two weeks allowed me to recharge and reflect. My fear was non-existent, and I rediscovered my child-like wonder. I met so many incredible souls who reminded me that people are good, kind, and genuine. People who reminded me who I am, and who I want to be. People who reminded me that life doesn't have to be taken so seriously and that I can do whatever I want. There is no right or wrong way. Only you can decide that for yourself. Do what's best for you and forget all the people that tell you otherwise along the way.

Galway felt like home to me. I was so full of life and love. There were often times when I found myself smiling or tearing up because of the joy I felt. It felt so right being there that it made me think back to the fear I felt booking my trip. To think I almost didn't go. One of the biggest barriers you could ever overcome in life is the fear and self-doubt you let constantly determine how you live your life. Fear is your ego trying to keep you in this imaginary bubble I like to call your "comfort zone." Fear is not your friend; don't let it trick you into thinking otherwise.

That being said, not *all* fear is bad. I mean, some fear keeps you alive and in one piece. There is good fear and bad fear, and some fear is just straight up irrational. Regardless, fear plays a huge role in all our lives. It will *always* be there, so acknowledge it. Respect it even, and then turn around and tell it to go away. Then do yourself a favour and go and do whatever it is you wanted to do anyway. When you decide not to do something you're scared of doing, ask yourself if it's because you genuinely don't want to do it, or if it's because your fear is keeping you from doing it. Overcoming that fear and doing it anyway could be the best decision you ever make. How else could we find that love that everyone longs for, or see the world, or land our dream job? So do it, whatever it may be. Whatever comes to mind for you, whether it is asking that guy out, or booking a trip, or maybe going to school! If you choose not to do something out of fear of what other people may think, then you've already failed. Life can be hard enough as it is; don't make it harder on yourself. Do what you need to do for you.

After getting home from Ireland, I realized that my biggest struggle wasn't finding a job and getting back into a routine. My biggest struggle was holding onto who I was when I was in Ireland—not letting fear consume me, not letting my stress run my life, and holding onto that desire I had for adventure and life. My pursuit of life started when I went halfway across the world on my own, but it doesn't have to be like that for everyone. Your life doesn't start when you get your dream job, or find the love of your life, or start a family, or go travelling. Your life is happening right now. It's already started, so stop waiting, stop making excuses. Do the best you can with what you've got, because life is too short. Hold onto the little things, whether it is your morning cup of coffee or spending Sunday afternoon with the people you love. Get outside, pay attention to the way the sun feels on your skin, and take note of the colours around you. Fall in love with life, every little detail. Fall in love with yourself.

When my dad asked me to write a chapter for his book, I wasn't sure what I'd write, or what I'd even have to offer anyone. Ireland changed me. That trip helped me grow. I never would have figured any of this stuff out if I hadn't acknowledged my fear and gone on the trip anyway. I never would have found my place in Galway. Okay, I shouldn't say never ... chances are I would have, but maybe not until much later in life. My only regret would be not doing this sooner. There are no words that really capture what Galway has done for me, what Ireland has done for me. One of my biggest questions when I was leaving was, "How do you capture a feeling?" My dad had the best response: "Only with your heart." So capture every feeling you have with all of your heart; own it and embrace it. The good and the bad. You have the ability to create whatever narrative you want for your life, so make it good and make it interesting! Don't you dare take the back seat to your own life, because when it comes down to it, life is just one crazy, beautiful adventure waiting to be had. Pursue it; don't just let it happen to you.

Be unapologetic in your pursuit of life.

RADICAL ENTRY 11

The Race

The race isn't a game; it's your life. Have you ever heard the tale of the old Cherokee of the two wolves? It goes like this:

> An old Cherokee was teaching his grandson about life. "A fight is going on inside me," he said to the boy. "It's a terrible fight between two wolves. One is evil—he is anger, envy, sorrow, regret, greed, arrogance, self-pity, guilt, resentment, inferiority, lies, false pride, superiority, and ego. The other is good—he is joy, peace, love, hope, serenity, humility, kindness, benevolence, empathy, generosity, truth, compassion, and faith. The same fight is going on inside of you and inside of every other person, too."
>
> The grandson thought about it for a minute and then asked his grandfather, "Which wolf will win?"
>
> The old Cherokee simply replied, "The one you feed."[3]

I've had a lot of experience feeding the wrong wolf. To make it worse, I felt justified because of the abuse I was subjected to. At certain times I felt entitled to how I was feeding this wolf. I had every right to feel sorry

---

[3] "Two Wolves," Virtues for Life: The Heart of Everyday Living, accessed March 7, 2018, https://www.virtuesforlife.com/two-wolves/

for myself. I became an expert at feeding the wrong wolf. I excelled at pushing the limits of the negative mental and physical manifestations outlined by the old Cherokee. I wasn't an evil person, but I wasn't great to be around either. I chose to be the person who fed the negative wolf. I couldn't do anything about the abuse until I was old enough to stop it. I can see that day as clearly now as when it happened. Standing up for that helpless little boy felt good. The pain didn't stop, and many issues were just beginning. Later as an adult, I could choose how to respond to those issues. For a time, I chose to increase and multiply all the negative, and that became the energy of my life.

I wasn't running a good and purposeful race. I was dead—living dead, feeling dead. There was no racing death. The race I was running was one that would have led to death if not for the intervention of God. When we feed the wrong wolf, we become blind. Actually, all of our senses are dulled. The enemy thrives on that mindset and fills us with his lies. To run the proper race, I needed to first see the lies and my own feeding frenzy.

THE INSANITY ARCHITECTS

Many of the physical feats we accept and think are normal today were once considered unachievable, even insane. The list is pretty impressive: the four-minute mile, a woman running a marathon (Can you believe women weren't even allowed to compete?), and swimming the English Channel. Events like Ironman and Ultramarathons were dreamt up and considered insane and beyond human limitations. Many thought that these events were dangerous and for the delusional. Now we are on the cusp of a sub two-hour marathon. To accomplish that will be a phenomenal human achievement, and I hope it happens within my lifetime. It's cool for me to think about people sitting around and coming up with the Ironman concept.

I was drawn to competing in Ironman and Ultramarathons because they seemed crazy. I knew that when I entered these events they were able to be accomplished, yet there was still an element of insanity. To take on an Ironman race was exactly how I was going to move my own needle and get to the other side of the "which wolf to feed" legend. It led me to allow God to lead me through the process of not conforming to this world. Radical is often stuck in our minds for a reason. It enters our psyche to release the wrong perceptions, views, and ways we have come to see as real which are actually just societal norms. I think that's one of the draws of these races—the insanity it takes to finish alters a person's mindset.

I applaud and am thankful for these architects of insanity. The people who create these events aren't just taking life as it comes—no, these folks are writing the history of life. What they saw as achievable and viable the rest of the world looked at as crazy. Crazy is relative when it comes to achieving a goal or dream. That's what racing death is all about. Up your crazy energy and smash the status quo. Enter into the realm of unreality that society defines, the realm of unreal which is real to the architects of insanity, which is the realm where you never allow a limiting mindset to shape or alter your Vision. Be the architect of your insanity to create a better pursuit lane. Besides, who defines what is insane and what is not?

OWNERSHIP

I certainly knew it was wrong, but everyone else was doing it, so I'm not to blame for my actions. A big part of my job is cleaning up after grown adults—people who agree to do a job that is well defined, well paying, and has very few expectations, but who simply can't do what they've entered into agreement to do. This word that I am about to write really needs to be revisited in how it is defined: accountability. I need to clarify that I work with many amazing people who do their jobs with great accountability and are professional in all manners. When your job entails dealing with the people who couldn't care less about their work and feel beyond entitled, you see how accountability wanes.

It's liberating to admit you've done the wrong and be accountable for it. Being a human means making mistakes. They are all a part of the experience of life. We grow and learn by making mistakes. In today's society when people make mistakes, many will not take ownership, and in this politically correct climate, they're not held accountable. In your pursuit of life, taking ownership for all you do can be the most powerful tool you build. Racing death should lead to an attitude of pursuing excellence. You're mental, physical, emotional, and spiritual actions should all aim at excellence. We know that perfection is an unattainable wasteland. Excellence is attainable, yet many levels of society settle for mediocrity. We allow for the attitude that just showing up is enough. If a person shows up 70 per cent of the time, we applaud how good that is. Your effort sucks, you're rude, and you don't work well with others, but here's your paycheque. Keep up the mediocre work. I think that should be the slogan for today: "Keep up the mediocre work; we don't expect any more from you."

If you're employed by a company or individual, this is what you need to do. Think like an owner. When you break it down, you really are the owner. You are the owner of your work ethic, so define it in terms of quality and commitment. Be as quick to own your mistakes as you are to own your accomplishments, and don't ever take credit for the work or ideas of others. Running this race requires authenticity in our actions, which come from being an agent of taking ownership. Willingly make ethical choices and decisions, even in the face of adversity. You can never look back with regrets about owning your life; it will help you race death. Your behaviour will dictate your level of success in anything you do. Learn to own the truth. Once you understand that truth, decide to live your Vision, and life will open up for you. I've played sports with, trained with, raced with, and watched athletes who were not the most talented or genetically qualified to rise to the top. And I have seen the opposite—talent that never attains the level it should. Grit up and take ownership of all you do and make your behaviour a thing of action and accountability.

METRICS

You've probably seen the bumper sticker, "He who dies with the most, wins." You're still dead—whatever you had, you're still dead. How you measure your life is up to you. I've never seen a hearse with a luggage rack. I want to measure my own success by how many people I serve over the course of my life. Inspiring, motivating, or helping them find or live their Vision is the coolest. Knowing that I've been a part of another person achieving a goal is my greatest joy. If someone has enough trust in me to coach or mentor them on their journey to a goal, then that's an amazing honour. I try my best to serve them with all of my heart.

The dance of life should include doing for those who can't or haven't got enough. Many of our problems in life can be overcome if we change the metrics of how we define and measure success and failure. No one can tell you how you should live. No one should dictate how you define success, and we should never accept a definition that goes against what works for us. Having people influence how we look at success is not a bad thing. We can learn from these metrics and see if they bring value into our lives; however, no one should try to influence how you define success or try to steer you away from what you know is true and in your own best interest. Too often well-meaning people try to influence our lives based on their views, opinions, and perspectives. Usually we discover that it really isn't what we should have done or gotten into. They meant no harm; they just had a different perspective than one that aligned with our Vision. This is a great exercise in self-discovery and defining what's really important. Taking time to seek out what really is success in your Vision can help steer your life in some cool and more satisfying directions.

I have very specific objectives that I aim for and a set form of metrics that I use to measure my success. These metrics keep me from conforming to the world. Yes, certain of my metrics have worldly permutations; I don't shun the ways of the world in all areas. I just don't chase the metrics that I see defined in advertising, media, and on many levels of life's conditioned values. I move to the wavelength of my own drums, and I beat what I can out of myself that I just don't want. I'm willing to suffer in order not to follow the path that society deems as successful, while at the same time aiming to not harm other people. My metrics are designed for me, to be achieved by me, and to be as harmless to my environment as possible. If I can achieve them, I'm following my true nature. If I can't, I need to examine if they are of value or if I'm unwilling to give up some unnecessary aspect of myself or my life to achieve them. The attainment of these metrics is important to all I do and drives the future for me. Take stock of how you measure success. Be aware of not just floating through the societal measures that may not have any value for you or may be harming what you value. A conscious awareness of these personal metrics creates the ability to achieve success that comes with the added value of joy. You are the master of you. Your metrics have great personal ramifications, so be kind and exuberant in your pursuit of them.

SIMPLE MINDED

There was a time when I wanted to be a complex and deep individual. In my younger years, I thought living in complex theories and philosophies was the way to journey. Having all sorts of information and science would help me to live a better, more interesting life. I learned some great stuff that's been useful in my pursuit, but I didn't pursue life as much as knowledge and complexity. I was interested in trying to know it all and be it all— a renaissance man of sorts. The truth is that I am limited. There are only so many subjects we can master. To truly master something is a time consuming and energy consuming pursuit. We won't be able to master it all, even with an immense intelligence.

Racing endurance events doesn't require complex plans. I discovered that the more complex I made the training and race day plan, the more things could go wrong. I adopted a simple-minded approach to my training and racing. I've put in place things I've learned over time through trial and error, but they've been simplified by me in every means possible to allow my mind to focus on minimalistic objectives to achieve success in the event.

To think that all of the information in this book would be applicable to you and achievable in your life is naïve on my part. That's why I call it a "to do" book. Do what works for you. Keep it simple, because that will be effective. If something is ineffective, it's a waste of time. Complexity looks fantastic, but does it equate to being effective? Not always, and that means more time trying to troubleshoot or find solutions.

Measuring devices for fitness are becoming more complex. They measure steps, calories burned, heart rate, power, and heaven knows what else. I've found that athletes who use these devices lose a sense of connection with themselves and their bodies. Their reliance on the technology makes them so dependent, they're unable to gain a sensory perspective on how to feel during physical activity. I use some technology, but I believe that the human body is a better measure of what's really going on to improve performance. Besides, when I'm out running or riding, I like to look around at the beauty of the world rather than something attached to my wrist.

Simplicity of thinking and mental processes is more powerful when you're creating and pursuing your Vision. My Vision used to have all these complex objectives and information. Yes, the more detailed we can be about these things the more likely we'll be able to achieve them, but complex doesn't mean more achievable. We can have very powerful objectives and ways to move continually in their direction. The KISS method (not KISS, the band) is a great reminder of this philosophy: Keep It Simple Stupid. When we can simplify something to be effective, that's a great accomplishment in mastery. To master a way to achieve something with the least amount of energy rocks. When it comes to work, I'm a minimalist and want to get it done now and not have it lingering over me. By creating a simple-minded approach to pursuing, we move our energy more efficiently and effectively. Become hard-core, simple minded, and master that which you know is going to move your needle.

RADICAL ENTRY 12

The Final Score

hat's the final score? Are we keeping track? Should we be keeping track? I really hope that we all are. Not as in a competitive state of keeping score, but keeping score of our lives to inspire the masses, our children, acquaintances, friends, peers, and hopefully complete strangers as well. In doing all of this, we hopefully inspire ourselves with the impact we have on the world. My hope is that somewhere in this book you found some tools or inspiration to help you move your own needle. Endurance is critical to an amazing life. We need to endure the bad things in life that are inevitable. Those bad things are challenges that help you solidify your Vision. Own the opportunity you have no matter where you are right now.

You'll need to define pursuit in your own terms, in terms of your own beliefs without any guilt. I've not provided any formula for you, because this is a personal quest. Any formula I create will be skewed. It will limit you in your own pursuit, as my formula is designed for me. What I have provided are some experiences, some of the tools I've had success with, and a lot of different information for you to ponder. There will be stuff in here that may resonate with you and hopefully inspire you. At the same time, there may be stuff in here you'll think is just garbage. I wrote things to challenge the status quo, things that have worked for me.

Pushing the boundaries is important to me but may not be for you. Just don't live dead, please. Scrutinize everything I've written and critique it. Move it around and dissect it sentence by sentence. Eliminate what doesn't work for you, and question all of it. Yell and scream at it if you need to in order to find the truth in it for you—if it's there. Allow the energy of the writing into your mind and allow your heart to thoroughly filter the message contained in it. Open your eyes and look around you to see if it has any value to your pursuit. I don't just want blind faith and non-discerning minds to mimic it. Either there's value for you, or there isn't. If you find value, now the real works begins.

Embrace this work of yours, this pursuit, as a vocation. A vocation can be described as a strong inclination to a particular course of action or state of being. Your state of being should be the top priority of your conscious mind daily. The etymology of vocation can be traced back in the French language to "vocacion" and broken out as "spiritual calling." In Latin it's derived from nominative vocation, which literally stands for "being called." In any work I do, I put myself first. At first glance that may seem like a selfish statement, but if I'm not interested in the work, I'm going to suck at it. If I don't put myself first and have the passion or energy needed, then forget about being of any value to you or anyone I'm working with. I am my first vocation, called by God to walk in His ways. As a vocation, I am committed to exploring fully the purpose I was designed to pursue and living it out in all the ways I am capable of. This is what being a disciple means to me. Magic happens when we are in pursuit of life. Magic is awesome, and I keep score of it all.

ATTACK LIFE

Life ain't waiting on you. Life has better things to do than worry about whether you're going to step up and act. Have fun with the mindset that you just need to wait for the right moment, because so many moments are just going to flow under the bridge. Financially you just need to get a little more in the bank, and then you'll start. You just need to wait until your children are a little older. The weather today isn't the kind you like to exercise in. All those things will hold you back, because they're just excuses. The timing is never right, and you're alright with that because it gives up control … and that is easy. It's the "averse to risk" mentality that the status quo leverages against us. It's limiting and debilitating when we decide what is worth pursuing. There is an action verb I use to combat it: attack! Moving into an attack mindset isn't difficult, and it's a reasonable way to be.

Attacking doesn't have to be aggressive or the use of force. I got a kick looking up the etymology of the word "attack" on etymology.com. What stood out was that it quite simply meant "to begin taking action." I will now and forever proclaim that the greatest force multiplier in our lives is daily action focused toward our objectives. There are large and small-scale attacks. Neither one works greater than the other. What really works is committing to the attack. Any kind has great potential.

There can be many beneficiaries of your attacks. First and foremost, you stand to benefit most from charging into the fray of your battle. There are two choices to weigh here as you ponder attacking. One, you can watch the battle from the back of the caravan and stay safe. Two, you can lead the charge and smile like a banshee as you impose your energy on life and pursue your Vision.

Life itself is benevolent. It is the system, and other humans that will try to stop or sway your attack. Life says, "Bring it on, because I'm for you." Life doesn't discriminate or hold you down. Circumstance may challenge you, but they don't dictate anything unless you give them permission to. You control only one thing in this life—you! That is one of our greatest battles, and one we need to attack every day. Don't try to control anything else; release control of all that you have no power over. You'll free up immense energy to live your Vision. By making this choice, you'll take a step toward mastering yourself, and your sphere of influence will be far- reaching.

I use the quiet attack method in my life. I work to raise others up and inspire them. Taking action on behalf of others is a great way to attack life daily. When I do this, the benefits I receive are tenfold. People give freely of their energy, which helps me gain strength in myself. I enjoy doing things for others to help them build their pursuit lanes, and I build stock in life as I do. When I'm in the act of helping others, my mind is quiet and I'm open to the spirit in my heart. Now I'm attacking life on a deeper level. This level of living is hard to attain by focusing solely on my own needs. The battles of others are a good way to create solutions in your own battles. Pursuit is an effort to secure or obtain a way, an objective, and a desired outcome. Attacking in our life creates action to obtain the objectives you know are necessary for living in pursuit. Training and racing have taught me one valuable lesson: you cannot achieve an outcome in a race without attacking your training. Compartmentalization of life is a barrier to success. Align all of your actions with your Vision. Attack that Vision with abandon and make it exuberant.

GET OUT IN FRONT OF IT

A principle I've learned in long distance races is to get my mind out in front of the distance. Learning to make peace with going the distance is key to wrapping the mind around how it's going to feel. In these races, you're more than likely going to feel physical and mental pain. Getting out in front of it prepares you for when it happens. It needs to be part of training, and it takes work. Distance is a real value, and pain is a real value. Overcoming them both is a quality one can build.

"Out in front of it" means you're willing to go where many people aren't. Sometimes as a coach you overstate the obvious over and over again. Long distance races are similar to life; after all, life is an endurance event. Training for the tough circumstances in races ups the quotient for success. I find that it either comes down to being reactive or responsive. When something negative happens, we want to respond. Responding comes from a place of preparation, from having control over our own emotions and actions. Responding is a way to come at the negative from a place of possibility.

"Out in front of it" means living in the moment at its finest. By getting your mind out in front of something, you've already created the moment. It's a time warp, and now you're living in that moment again. Repetitive training is getting out in front of it. Teaching the body and mind to act without thinking builds the pathways for the mind to allow the body to respond. We have created the moment of response before we've even lived it. This is taking control to a different level and understanding how we can impact our future. In the event that we have to react, those reactions don't come from an emotional place. Responses have been rehearsed over and over through training. That is spot on "get out in front of it" training and racing.

BUILDING THE TEMPLE

Where do you worship? Our ways and means of worship dictate our health and well-being. Do you worship your car or home? Maybe your work? I have to make a point to focus on where I should be focusing my worship, because I get distracted by stuff I shouldn't be focusing on, such as my job, things out of my control, and other unnecessary things. Bad things happen if I roll too far down that rabbit hole.

Worship for me starts with building my own temple, starting right here in my own inner back yard, in every action, word, thought, and way. The fountain of truth starts inside and works its way to the outside. The standard in society is usually the other way around, but we're best to create it from the inside. The "temple first" mentality is really different, because we're indoctrinated in ways that create the opposite effect in our lives. We're made to believe that dependence on the government and other institutions is best for us. There's a need in society to worship things outside of ourselves. Our inner temple became an option when Jesus chose the cross for us. The ability to build the temple comes from one choice—to honour that one death with the life we pursue. We're offered a path of radical pursuit if we choose to be brave and free. Our root decision will dictate our choices, our focus, our dedication, and our discipline. Building a solid temple on the cornerstone of what the cross offers is freedom. The opposite is slavery to the ways of this world and living the status quo, something you follow out of conditioning.

Choosing the inner temple and building it daily is the root choice of our pursuit. We have within us great hope, built into our cells, and from it comes immense faith that we will have inner peace, and that we're living a great plan that includes all of humanity gaining that inner peace. The way to build an amazing temple from the inside out is self-love. We are our own worst critics and destroyers of our self-esteem. We live in a society so driven by an outer version of how we should be that it destroys people.

Life doesn't keep tabs on looks and material possessions. Life keeps score on true nature. Nature offers us great examples of how we can build our temple. Nature is the opposite of societal conditioning, which is controlling, designed to stunt individualism, and hungry for recognition based on its wants and needs. Nature is our true nature, shining in reality for us to witness. Nature is the foundation of life, and we are wise to recognize that reality. Pursuing outside your inner temple will leave you feeling lost and without hope. A faith-based inner pursuit of the true temple within will fill you with hope, and then faith has the power to move mountains.

The temple is real; it is now, and it is the light in which we can walk. Today is the first day of the rest of your life. It is the first day of building your temple and taking action in pursuit of your Vision. It is the first day to fall in love with you and with life. You are loved more than you know by God. God keeps no score, and He doesn't want anything but kingdom living for you. He is the temple seed waiting to be watered and to grow in ways that benefit and embolden you to pursue life. Happy temple building! Be alive and aware. Thanks for being you.

The Random Effect

I had so much material for this book, I had to cut it down. I put these ideas here under "random." I like to be random in my training and thinking, so this made sense. This is a collection of things I use in my pursuit lanes that have made my life better.

REDIRECT

When I took my martial arts training, I learned the importance of redirecting. An important principle in the arts is how to redirect an opponent's energy. Only as a last resort would one want to meet force with force, direct energy with direct energy. I was recently reminded of the great power of the act of redirecting. Mentally redirecting can be a great weapon when racing death. We often try to meet force with force, but that kind of mental energy is a draining. When our thoughts wander to negative things, we need to redirect our mental energy.

During an endurance event (remember, life is an endurance event), many things can go wrong. If things start to go wrong mentally, it can mean a lot of pain. I'm talking about mental duress. Brick walls are hard to crash through head-on. Learning to redirect bad mental energy will make a difference in life. This is an important skill to learn in any area of your life. Nothing you do physically will overcome a bad attitude. A bad attitude is like weeds growing in a garden; they take over and choke out the valued growth. The exact same principle applies in your mind.

To redirect mental energy takes awareness and practice (deliberate.) You need to make yourself aware of the anchors that mentally pull you into a force versus force play. It may be self-judgement, bad self-talk, or complaining. You need to be honest and look deep into your mind to find the weeds. Starting this process can cause you to get down on yourself. Take a step back and remember why you're working on this. Beating yourself up isn't going to further your ability to redirect your mental energy. Be objective and truthful with an attitude bent on moving into a redirect mindset.

When you're feeling mentally crushed or in a bad state, focus on some deep breathing. Take your focus and start some cyclical, deep breaths. Focus on allowing the breath to fill your lungs so you're not shallow breathing. Air is our primary source of fuel and energy. Focusing on our breathing stimulates the parasympathetic nervous system, which in turn helps redirect that mental energy. As you change the shape of your body with the breath, you can redirect and change the shape of your mind and mental energy. Gaining composure through the practice of deliberate breathing creates a shift in the chemistry of your brain. It calms your brain by allowing peace to enter.

Now take the energy of your mind captive and focus your mental energy on Vision objectives. This gives you complete control over your mental energy. Having the ability to mentally direct energy will increase your ability to pursue life.

DISEASES OF BEHAVIOUR

There comes a point of clarity where we understand which of our habits are good and which are bad. We figure out the habits that move us in the direction of our Vision. We know which ones we should attach our pursuit to. These are the ones we feel good about, and they move the spirit. What cowards we become when pushed to create change in limiting habits!

Diseases of behaviour are real and challenging. I've found that the majority of people I encounter know the changes they want to make in their lives. They understand how the habits they want to change limit them, yet the majority will never move past those limiting habits. The reason is simple—comfort. Comfort is the greatest symptom of diseases of behaviour, but it's not the final diagnosis. These diseased behaviours have become so comfortable, they're a habit.

Comfort doesn't care if it's good for you or if it's killing you! Comfort doesn't want change. If it means creating change, comfort will rebel. Comfort is a very powerful force with its own gravitational pull. We all have an inner drive and desire for comfort; society knows this and leverages it to gain control over us. Society holds comfort as one of its greatest values. We have elevated comfort to the level of personal entitlement. For the most part, our lifestyles are comfortable.

To recognize that a behaviour is diseased creates a tipping point. Awareness allows you to start moving away from the habit. To cure any behaviour, just commit to simple actions daily that will override the habit. Make the energy of being uncomfortable with the diseased behaviour greater than your comfort level. Build such discomfort into the habit that it becomes easy to redirect the energy into a habit you want. Build the new habit from the roots up by creating a sense of urgency. I describe it as "your back against the wall" strategy. Act as if the diseased behaviour you want to change is killing you. It fact, it just might be doing that. Use the fear, anger, frustration, and dislike of the habit to motivate you to create change.

Diseases of behaviour are conditioned into us; we have to be a willing participant in the disease. You need to be a willing participant in your own healing. Get so uncomfortable with your comfort level that it creates energy of actionable movement and change.

A VOICE CRYING IN THE WILDERNESS.

Neither John the Baptist nor Jesus had an ornate, palatial building to preach in. They both lived austere lifestyles and spoke to people wherever they came to them. Today the Christian experience, in my estimation, comes under a predetermined mold. Can somebody mix it up and break the mold? The mold has become moldy. The church is not a building or all the money that goes into it. The church is an infinite voice about the

Love of God. I couldn't care less about the building I'm in when I hear the message. What I want is a message that explodes me from the inside with passion and fuel to find God in every minute. I should leave and walk up to every person I meet and share the Good News.

Every Sunday feels like deja vu. The Christian model is based on money, and its true form has become lost in man's interpretation. We really need to take a look at this. Doing some research, I discovered that many families can't afford the tithe they give to their churches, but churches keep springing up all over the place. Many are getting bigger and bigger. Some of these pastors make big cash, putting their kids through the best colleges while these families that can't afford to are putting money into the coffers. Still every week we hear how important the tithe is. I'm not saying don't tithe, but where does it say that the tithe all has to go to the church? This is the standard approach we see in Christianity. Give your tithe to the church, because we do God's work. I know churches that are truly making great differences in their communities, but the church shouldn't be a money-making business.

God doesn't care if I'm in a building when I worship Him. As a matter of fact, I feel a greater presence of the Holy Spirit when I'm running or biking in nature. I've searched many churches for that same feeling, but usually it's just different wrapping around the same old same old. I prefer going to the mountains to really meet with the Spirit. I'm looking for that voice crying out in the wilderness, not the temple priests with their duplicity. Give me an experience that moves the spirit in me and is a knock-me-down-drag-me-out lesson.

Being a Christian isn't something we do for a couple hours on Sunday, nor is it making sure that we're tithing! Don't just show up ... be that voice for change and the one shouting out from the wilderness all about the Good News. It's not weird or wrong to feel that your church isn't providing you with what you need for your journey. Simply staying the course for the sake of the church does you no good. Be proactive in your journey and push your church to make this experience fully about the Spirit and its disciples. Jesus was considered weird because He didn't follow the status quo. I love the example He set for us to follow.

Important note: tithing is important, and I do tithe. The issue I have with the tithe is that it shouldn't supersede the truth of the Good News. People should not be going into financial distress because they feel pressure to tithe.

BOLD

Being bold in life can put a target on your back. Go for it anyway! People really like to judge those who are bold enough to stand out or stand up. Being a stand-up person means being unfazed or not caring about people who judge you. Are you hurting anyone by standing up? Maybe you are. If you're hurting a bully by standing up, that's different. If people are being repressed and you stand up to the people doing the repressing, they may be hurt. We must stand up for morals and values.

Ours is a life of pursuing our Vision boldly, not fearing obstacles. Life gives you a choice: be bold or be a delicate flower. If you're waiting for the right person, time, or opportunity, your flower pot will be all you ever see or inhabit. Bold moves you out of a state of reliance into a state of resilience. You don't wait on life … you set the tone.

When I enter into a physical challenge, I don't ponder the pain or how hard it will be. I stand bold in my intention and conviction. The finish line is not the end; it is the beginning of the next challenge. The moment I sign up for the event, I have a choice: go hard and be prepared, or suck. I hate it when I suck and don't put in the effort. Being bold allows you to falter. Being bold allows you to get back up for the opportunity to atone.

Being bold requires an attitude of knowing you may get beaten up for who you are. Being bold often scares other people. Some people can't handle that others will stand up and go against the status quo of a lack of morals, values, and ethics. To them it's more important to have the title or position than it is to do the right thing. All you have to do is look around at the society we live in to see this. It takes a bold attitude to rise above the unhealthy world we've come to inhabit. Step out and help others by being bold enough to make a difference where you can.

COURAGE

"Success is never final; failure is never fatal. It's courage that counts."[4]

If I could be coached by one person, I'd be coached by John Wooden. He really was the epitome of a coach. When you look at the etymology of the word "courage," you'll discover that it's based on heart. Maybe that's a little misleading, because it concerns speaking one's mind through telling what's in your heart. That's the Latin origin of the word "courage." Most languages hold to a similar definition.

In today's world it can take great courage to speak your heart. Courage means stepping up and being full on honest with yourself and with life. There's a freedom when we step out in courage, which comes from freeing our nature. Courage can result in hardships. If the thought of hardship seems daunting, then I suggest you step right into it and live it. Backing down is not an option when you have a true nature that needs to be expressed. Life is beautiful, and in that beauty through courage we can find success in life as we define it.

We need to run toward the challenge. Challenges never go away; they just fade and eventually become regret. We are not people who will live with regrets. It's not part of our nature to turn our backs on a challenge. When we embrace fear for what it is, we will be able to rise up through courage and full on kick butt. Fear is a limiter, although it does have a purpose for self-preservation. I always caution against putting ourselves in danger ... that's a big part of wisdom. How many of the challenges we face in life will put us in harm's way? Doing an Ironman carries inherent risks, but they are all manageable, and with proper preparation they aren't even scary. We create unnecessary fear because we live in a comfort zone prescribed by society.

Courage is a force multiplier; it increases the probability that you will successfully achieve your objective. The most valuable lesson I've learned about taking on any challenge is to focus on the primary, not the secondary. It's easy to get caught up in the idea of mental multi-tasking, which usually diffuses our energy and creates an unfocused person. The primary focus needs to be on what will make you successful in this very moment of the challenge. Take action to create a mindset of primary

---

[4] Wooden, John. http://www.thewoodeneffect.com. Accessed June 4, 2018.

focus. Being fully present, fully engaged, and fully alive takes a fervent courage. Courage is within you; it's something you can foster and grow. Even if you fail, knowing that you faced the challenge with courage will lead to growth and eventual success.

ART, THE PERSONAL KIND

One of the greatest travesties in life occurs when personal art is not expressed. So many people I meet have songs unwritten, books unpublished, and paintings unfinished. Other things in life become more important than nurturing their own art. Fears of their own or those projected on them by others keep them from creating and shipping their art.

Just as sad is the lack of attention and dedication to making anything you do art. The human condition has become one of entitlement for our talents as opposed to our talents being our art. We pursue recognition for the sake of recognition, not for the value we bring to our propositions or expenditures. Where we make life art, we are rewarded accordingly. When we make life about what we deserve, we devalue our personal art. There's an abundance of ways to express these values. All of our circumstances may not be ideal in our own minds. Our art might be exactly what those circumstances we find ourselves in need. Stick with it, never quit, and always believe in yourself.

Inside of you through all of life's ups and downs is your art. This art was given to you and to you alone. Digging into that place in your heart and pulling that art free to express to the world takes courage. Your courage could save the world ... it really could. Who knows how your art could impact the world? We'll never know if you repress it. We need your art; the world needs it and is waiting for you to express it for all of us to experience it.

ABSTRACT THINKING

The surface can hide much deeper patterns and ideas. On the surface we may put on masks that hide the deeper-level person we truly are. We need to unmask ourselves, because wearing a mask that hides who we are is not racing death. We mentally process life through the mask, making it incorrect for our truth. We then become societal-conditioning thinkers who have lost our abstract way in the process of conforming. Thinking only on the surface limits how we process life, and that limits our pursuit.

Abstract thinking allows us to challenge the status quo, giving us more ways of taking back the control we need of ourselves. Our identity requires that we look under the surface for those things that we truly know match our energy and pursuit. Buying into the status quo doesn't have any value for the seeker. It keeps the patterns and lanes of pursuit locked into what is deemed to be important societally. The abstract thinker can undercut the non-reality that comes with a lot of this societal political correctness. Having a sense of purpose that doesn't meet the conditioning opens the abstract thought processes that allow us to move into true Vision and pursuit.

To think in the abstract is to connect with the undercurrent of life where energy flows freely. The energy that created all we see can be ours to tap into and flow with. The concrete mindset of the surface-built thinking of society tries to create a way of thinking that pulls us into that mindset. It wants to eliminate opposition to its thought value. Those who are pursuing their true nature see through this to the abstract truth of nature in life. Being guided by your true nature never allows you to be pulled above the surface. Funny, isn't it? Abstract thinking pulls us below the surface to the truth. You can shout out loud "I'm getting pull under" and be happy about it.

UNLIFE HACKS

Google "life hacks" and see how many times the word "easier" comes up. Make life easier. They will change your life. They will make your life a lot simpler. If you need to search "life hacks," you really just need to simplify your life. Life hacks is another great way to sell us the status quo and keep the great marketing wheel turning. The basis of life hacks is to remove the need to do the work, but that's not always effective. UNlife hacks are the opposite; they're about making your life harder. They're about getting back to being simple in mind, body, and spirit. Finding ways to eliminate the easy in pursuit of the hard is really a great way to free your mind.

Convenience can take over our lives, because it seems to alleviate some of life's stress by saving time. These life hacks continue to jump into the collective conscience as a way to make life easier and to save time. Remember how all of this technology was going to make our lives easier? I'm still waiting! The illusion of convenience has become a big part of societal conditioning driven by marketing. On the one hand, we have the driving force of materialism and the "more is better" mindset. Then we have the life hack industry trying to sell us more to minimize our discomfort. Buy more, because it will create ways for you to make more time for the things that really matter. Convenience is an easy thing to sell, and we're an easy mark ... until we discover that it's not working.

You may be surprised how much simpler your life will become when you choose to exchange convenience for a more difficult way. Explore the joy of riding a bike as a means of commuting as opposed to sitting in traffic and getting upset. Attack the notion that we need to make life easier and that all of these life hacks are the answer. Do the opposite— eliminate anything that brings no value to your life. Cut back on activities or commitments you don't want but feel obligated to do. This can be a really difficult thing to do, because we buy into the compromise mindset and feel guilty when we aren't doing them. We believe that easier is better, and that fitting more in makes us more productive and feel more important.

Challenge that mentality and simplify to the bare necessities your activities and how you spend your time. Seriously look at what isn't making your Vision a reality. Remove the comfortable excuse those wasted actions have become. In their place, schedule the actions you know are required to achieve the pursuit of your Vision. Embrace the jumping fear that will rise up and try to keep you locked into this secure and easy path. Hard is the beautiful path filled with lessons of value, growth, and triumph. Nothing worth having is ever easy to get. If it was, then it really wasn't all that important. Investment in uncomfortable is investment in building your temple. It is built on solid rock and with a solid cornerstone. The value of hardship is tangible and concrete. Easy is a marketing ploy we buy into.

UNlife hacks are not about making life easier but are designed to make your life more real and to help live your true nature. One reason I push myself in training and racing is because it's not easy. The objective is to make myself stronger through hard work and struggle. It would be easy to say, "Man, I've done enough of this stuff. I just want to make my life easier in this area." But my UNquenchable desire to see my real nature is far more important than what is convenient. Hacking what is hard and adding it to my way of training makes me excited, and the training stays fresh. I'm interested in taking the level of my life to the highest point I can and walking in the glory of my pursuit. You can't hack into Heaven.

Epic and Extreme

One of the greatest gifts we have as humans is the ability to show compassion and empathy and to help others. There are many wonderful ways in which we can pursue life through giving of our time and skills. The rewards are much greater than any financial awards or recognition we may receive. Life provides us a choice to serve others or to be self-centred. There are many ways to serve others. Volunteering, fundraising, and bringing awareness to charitable causes can really give us personal satisfaction in knowing that we've made a difference.

Life is an opportunity to live, to be alive, and to move energy in positive ways. We can seek that path that opens us to our ability to create hope. Hope is an open door we can show others by our actions—actions we can use to serve people who may be in need, down and out, or facing difficulties. Actions are not cheap. They show our true nature, our true love for other human beings. To act in service to others is one of life's greatest callings. We make a difference when we step into a void left in a life and act to serve. It can also be epic.

THE KIDS WITH CANCER SOCIETY

Kids get cancer, and that's a tragedy. I don't know why it happens. I don't understand it, but I can make a small difference and hopefully change things up. The statistics regarding families with a child diagnosed with cancer are frightening. When a child is diagnosed, life for the family changes drastically. In 80 per cent of marriages, one parent has to quit a job to be there for the treatments and recovery. The financial burden is tough, but the time required to care for the child and go through all the treatments dictates this action. Close to 50 per cent of marriages end in divorce because of the stress.

The Kids with Cancer Society provides over fifty programs to families to help them face this challenge they never chose. Money raised by the society goes directly to families to help with expenses that arise from the diagnosis. These programs are designed to help the entire family, because one child being diagnosed has an impact on the entire family unit. The society doesn't just provide help; they provide hope and a shoulder to cry on. They become a family member. The questions and uncertainty surrounding a diagnosis are daunting for the parents and extended family. The society helps them deal with this overload through their programs and the compassionate hearts of their amazing staff. These are special people, dedicated and filled with compassion. Having the chance to know these people is an awesome honour and pleasure.

THE TOUR OF HOPE

The Tour of Hope is an annual bike ride held in June that helps raise money for the society. It's one of their biggest fundraisers. Cyclists commit to riding seven or eight days and raising money for the cause. Amazing sponsors pay for the accommodations, food, and transportation, so all the money raised by the cyclists goes straight to the society. This means that the money raised goes directly to families.

When I heard about the tour, I was intrigued. As an athlete and person who likes a physical challenge, I wanted to take part in the tour. I love riding my bike, so to ride for an entire week was definitely of interest. It wasn't until I started to research what the society does that I went full in and registered for the 2015 ride. This is a ride that honours the kids and families helped by the society. When I registered, I had no idea the impact this event would have on my life. Only one thing was a little daunting—fundraising.

I'll come back to the Tour of Hope.

DAN'S TWENTY-FOUR-HOUR RIDE

Asking people to donate money is uncomfortable for me. People don't mind donating; I just feel uncomfortable asking. There are so many worthy causes and charities, so I needed an idea that was unique, different, and included a challenge. In June of 2015, I was going to be riding over 900 kilometres to earn the money people would donate to the society. Personally, I find that when you do something like the tour to raise funds, people get behind the idea. They see that you're putting in effort and time, and they respond. Adding the power of what the society does for children suffering from cancer helps sell the fundraising.

I wanted something that was going to get me close to or over the fundraising commitment quickly! My friend Dave and I had talked once about doing a twenty-four-hour endurance run for a charity. We discussed this idea as a means to push ourselves while at the same time serving others. Now it's important to know that Dave is not right in the head ... LOL.

I'll come back to Dan's twenty-four-hour ride.

EXIST CYCLE AND JAMIE

In early 2014, I met an energetic, cool, and inspiring cycle/fitness studio owner named Jamie. Jamie owns Exist Cycle/Exist Fitness in Sherwood Park, Alberta, where I live. Jamie was looking to start a triathlon club in her cycle studio. I'm a triathlon coach, so we were introduced.

Jamie and I had the same philosophy about training, racing, and what we'd like a triathlon club to be about. Our vision was for an inclusive group for every level of experience— from beginner right on up to well-seasoned triathletes. So that's what we started. We started the club in the early months of spring and set a goal for an early June race. The club has over twenty-five members as I write this. Our athletes have completed Half Ironman, Ironman, Olympic, and off-road races. The group has evolved into the Exist TRIbe. I've made some lifelong friends who I met through the club. Our lives together extend beyond just training and racing. We hold social events and are a great source of inspiration, motivation, and support for each other.

This was all made possible by Jamie and her amazing spirit. Jamie wants to help people succeed and accomplish their fitness goals. She's the most giving person I've met in the fitness industry. Many trainers are in it for the money and want to get recognized for their contributions to people's lives. Jamie has an amazing ability to move people into a position to become the best they can be in their current state of fitness. I can't speak highly enough of this beautiful person or the impact she's had on my life and the people of the TRIbe.

BACK TO THE TWENTY-FOUR-HOUR RIDE

As mentioned earlier, the Twenty-Four-Hour Challenge was something that had been contemplated in the past, except we'd thought about it as a running challenge. Now I thought, *Why not a cycling challenge? Could I ride a spin bike for twenty-four hours?* Maybe, just maybe this would be feasible. Exist Cycle had a spin bike; I could ride and ask people to pay and ride. They could ride as little or as long as they desired. Teams could enter to see how far they could ride in twenty-four hours. I turned this idea over in my mind, and I liked the possibilities.

I approached Jamie and her partner, Shelly—another phenomenal person—and asked if I could use their studio for twenty-four hours. I explained that it would be a fundraiser for the Kids with Cancer Society. Jamie and Shelly didn't hesitate; they offered the studio and got behind the ride. So Dan's Twenty-Four-Hour Ride was born. To ride continuously for twenty-four hours seemed questionable. I didn't think it possible to sit and pedal for that long and physically be able to meet the demands. I'd require bathroom breaks, clothing changes, and would need to fuel up. I decided that I would ride for two-hour intervals and then take a ten-minute break. This would provide an opportunity for changes and eating. I wondered if I was going to need a nap, so the ride would take closer to twenty-seven hours.

I was committed, so that meant having to plan. I had no idea what it would all look like or how to get people to attend. I had a poster designed that I could put up wherever I wanted, and I used social media to promote the ride. My TRIbe, the Exist Triathlon Club, jumped into the ride and decided that they'd have someone on a bike with me the whole time. I wouldn't have to ride alone, which wasn't something I'd even considered. My amazing wife, Shelley, organized a team as well, which was cool. Something unusual would take place over the time leading up to the ride ... it would take on a life of its own. As I think about it, I can't even remember who had the idea, but it was suggested that we secure raffle items that people could buy tickets for, with all proceeds going to the society. This added a whole new dimension to the event. People who didn't want to ride or who couldn't ride would be able to come in and support the event through the raffle.

The number of people who came to ride, visit, hang out, and donate was truly humbling. When the ride was over and the numbers totaled up, I'd raised over $7,000. People got behind the ride in ways I'd never even imagined. A member of Exist Cycle who owns a sandwich shop in Sherwood Park donated sandwiches to the event. Water was donated, people brought coffee and other snacks, and it just grew and was a special time.

I wanted the ride to be a challenge because of what families faced with the diagnosis of childhood cancer. If I suffered a little on a bike for twenty-four hours to raise some money and make a small difference, then it was worth it. What happened over that twenty-four-hour period is a testimony to the human spirit. Cancer survivors came and rode bikes, even if they'd not been on a bike for many years. Families came and rode or spent time mingling and meeting other families. I took my idea to a community, and that community came out and stepped up to make the idea a success. All I did was have an idea and ride a bike. People love to make a difference. I was overwhelmed by the support of friends, family, and people in my community I had never met before.

I've held this event now for three years. In 2018, it will be the fourth annual Twenty-Four-Hour Ride. It continues to grow and, most importantly, make money for the society. In the second year, one of the TRIbe members named Heather rode the whole twenty-four hours with me. Heather is an amazing athlete and person. She has Type 1 diabetes, but that doesn't stop her from running Ultra's, triathlons, and all sorts of amazing things. That's the community of people I'm blessed to hang out with and the people I call my friends

THE TOUR OF HOPE REVISITED

June of 2015 rolled around and I had my funds raised to ride in the Tour of Hope. I was trained and ready. I didn't know anyone who was taking part in the ride. I was a rookie and didn't fully know what to expect, but man was it exciting. There was a pre-ride meeting where I got to know some riders a little bit, so there was some familiarity. I had butterflies; I hadn't had butterflies for an event in a long time.

The first day we travelled from Edmonton, Alberta to Kelowna, British Columbia. We spent close to twelve hours on the road in a van. Conversation with people in my van was easy, and they all made me feel right at home and part of the team. Over the next seven days, I rode with cancer survivors and with people who had children who had used the services of the Kids with Cancer Society. Those cyclists were there to give back because of the immense value the society brings to families who need it. I rode with people who'd never had cancer in their lives, but someone in their lives had been affected by it. They rode because they wanted to make a difference for families in need. What an incredible group of people; it was an honour to be on this ride with all of them.

Volunteers came and supported us, some because they had a grandchild who'd needed the society. That's one of the realities of this terrible disease—it takes lives. When those victims are children, it really makes no sense. At night after our team supper we'd have a meeting about the next day's ride and logistics. It was also at these meeting where each rider and volunteer was asked to speak about why they participated in the ride. Some of the stories were heart wrenching, and many nights there weren't too many dry eyes in the place. For a rookie, it truly was an eye- opening experience.

On the final night before the ride ended on the Sunday, a young lady named Maria came and spoke to us about her cancer experience and how Kids with Cancer had helped her and her family. At fifteen years old she'd been through more than I'd ever experienced, and she was alive and well. Her speech was more than just moving … it was a tribute to all the children who have faced cancer, whether they survived or not. This was why I was riding—why we were riding. We rode to provide hope and a means for the society to help, to make a difference, to support.

That was a moment I'd never forget, and it was at that moment I knew I had to continue this ride.

Entering into this challenge, I had no idea how much of an impact it would have on me. Meeting all of the people I shared the experience with was more important than riding a bike. In 2017, I completed my third Tour of Hope. Every year it gets better and better. These people are now my riding family; they're my friends. I'm blessed to have been able to enter into such a worthy way to make a difference in this world.

A DENT IN THE UNIVERSE

Can you and can I make a difference in this world? Is it possible to see through all of the negativity and create something positive to help others? The answer is this: we were born to. It's part of what we were designed to do in the master plan. Humanity is one tribe; we're all connected through our hearts and the energy of our Creator, and we can make a dent in the universe. When we decide to look at things from a perspective of empathy and sympathy, our compassionate hearts rise up and create hope. We become a beacon for others who will find strength through us and our example.

As a member of the universal tribe, you have free license to move into a position as an agent of change in the world. Change agents move and they take action. It's their energy moving outside of the normal plain of the self that creates a dent in the universe. Sometimes on the outside there is no thanks, no kudos. Inside, where it matters most, you'll be changed and know that you made a dent. There's more value in working to create hope, to make a difference for those who can't, than in any outward rewards. When you put forth energy to help the afflicted or those in need, your heart makes a connection with God. That is where real rewards are created.

That is how you make a dent in the universe. God has infinite love for His creation. You and I were designed to connect with and feel that love directly and intimately. As you step up within the tribe to sacrifice a portion of your own loving energy, God bends the universe to help you make a difference. We may not understand how the dent impacts others or even ourselves, because God has a greater plan that we can't always see. We have the ability to trust, though, and use faith to make that dent. When we trust God, He moves in, around, and through us to create that dent.

Being an agent of change is fulfilling, although it may take time and effort to find the area in which you can create change. Don't allow societal conditioning to take away the power within you to be an agent of change. Listen to the guidance of the Spirit and move into what works for you, not what others think is best for you. I never thought I could create something like the Twenty-Four-Hour Ride and have it be this successful. Our own mind can cloud the area we really need to focus on to make our dent. Be extreme and epic in your search for that special gift that is yours to make a dent in the universe.

LIFE ALTERING

It's funny how these events have become life altering for me. I've completed the Tour of Hope and my Twenty-Four-Hour Ride for three consecutive years. In 2017, the Ride was the most grueling to date for me. Up until this year, I'd never struggled mentally with the event. It's always challenging, but I'd never felt like it was ever in jeopardy of not getting done by me. Not so much this year. I struggled desperately from around 4:00 a.m. until 8:00 a.m. It was the closest I'd ever come to packing it in on the Ride, and I still had a long way to go. How would that work if the dude who was supposed to ride quit? I had some great riders during those hours with me on whom I could focus to keep my mind from faltering. I had a picture of my sponsor child from the society tapped to the wall beside me. I'd ridden two years in a row for Porter, who is six years old. When I was at my lowest point during the twenty-four hours, I'd look at Porter. How difficult was what I was doing compared to what this little dude had been through in his young life? Porter had been diagnosed at two years old. His little smiling face was what I focused on to make myself not quit.

I can't cure cancer, but I can make a difference through these two events, and these two events have impacted other people. Having your life altered in a way that makes you feel like you're making a difference is so powerful. There are many amazing organizations and societies in need of volunteers. Step into the void and maybe your life will be altered in epic ways you never knew possible.

I WANT TO BE RIDICULOUS

I picture myself in my eighties running half marathons and marathons. I picture myself still dressing in tights with shorts over top and wearing a hoody on cool fall days. I picture myself going for two-hour rides with a huge smile on my face and massive joy in my heart. I want to be ridiculous in my pursuit of life no matter how old I am, because that's what life is all about. I want to look into the eyes of death and know that I did it my way and was happy doing it. I don't care what other people think of me; their opinions and conditioning have no power over how I will pursue life. Who defines what is ridiculous and what isn't? Don't answer that, as it's a rhetorical question. As long as my pursuit doesn't harm other people, anyone can judge it ridiculous and I don't care.

We spend a lot of time in our early years worrying about what others think of us. Actually, it can be a lifetime distraction. We want to fit in, and society pressures us to be like others. I know, because I did it. It was hard to be myself and still try to fit in. That was a perspective issue as opposed to an issue of reality. I gave in to peer pressure, which was a choice. It's a tough struggle our youth face. Man, that was a lot of energy and time spent on stuff that really wasn't me. I can look back on it and chuckle now, but I'm not going to waste energy any more on being politically correct when it isn't correct or morally right. I'll stand up to injustice, but my energy doesn't extend to agendas that aren't truly based on values. I can't help it if people don't like my way or what I write or stand for. As long as I'm not harming others, I will continue my pursuit.

My ridiculous is pure energy that drives me forward in my pursuit, and it is joy. Joy isn't something to subdue just because others judge your joy. If they're judging you, that means they're focusing on you and not their own way. What a waste to squander energy on trying to create others in our own image! We were created in the image of God, so focus on that. When I lay my head to rest the final time, I hope that I've run my ridiculous-meter completely empty. I have no desire to withhold my true nature any more in this lifetime. I love how powerful being involved in a ridiculous goal makes me feel. The power of inner energy that fuels my pursuit comes from a ridiculous attitude and mindset. To be cautious is prudent; to allow caution to subdue your latent ridiculous self is not cool.

Rise up in energy to your Vision so you will never feel as though you could have done more. It's your truth that's on the line right now. Take control of your energy in a way that pulls all doubt out of your life. You've got time and ability, so why not create a ridiculous attitude and live from it? Really, what do you have to lose? Nope, check that. A better question to ask ourselves is: What do we have to gain?

UN IN ACTION

I'm going to share with you a couple of resources that I have used for myself and with clients. We are UNearthing our true nature. To pursue life, we start by going on an archeological dig to search for our true nature buried beneath all the conditioning that piles up over the years. We are at the core of our radical pursuit.

We are going to build ourselves some EUTM:

A) Enthusiasm Unknown to mankind
B) Energy Unknown to mankind.

We've discovered that societal conditioning can be limiting and unhealthy and can keep us from living our truth. We have to make a choice. We can stay the course and live in the moment as we're conditioned to do, or we can live UN, doing the excavation work and releasing ourselves from the rubble of that conditioning. If you're truly happy with the status quo, that's cool, and you don't need this. But if you want a change, we can rip apart the status quo and build a lifestyle that suits our specific needs and one that supports our Vision.

UN means to remove from, release from, free from, or to do the opposite of. With UN we can reverse all of the limiting beliefs and unnecessary boundaries that societal conditioning has built up in us. UN enables you to move forward and own your pursuit of life.

UN Training Tenet: To Break the Chains of Normal and the Curse of Mediocrity.

UN is a personal operating system. As your personal operating system, UN enhances your ability to manage yourself. Remember, all we can control is ourselves. When we're able to manage ourselves, we're in a position to create a lifestyle of deliberate practise to carry us along on this pursuit to our Vision. At its core, UN is designed to help you achieve your objectives. Whether for healing, lifestyle, fitness, relationships, or any other aspect of your life you want to recreate, UN can help.

Why does UN work? Because in the process of working through this UN, we work toward personal mastery. The word "master" can refer to the title given to the original of a recording, which brings us back full circle to the reason we want to remove the veil of societal conditioning from our own selves. You have within you the master plan, and that will never be erased. The Master who planned everything created that original recoding specifically for you, and then gave you possession of the Spirit to help you understand and fulfill the Vision of the Master recording. The Master recording is so much greater than any of the conditioning that has worked to try and cover over it.

Self-mastery is the stumbling block many people have to face in order to live out UN in their lives. We all have our habits and weaknesses that create consternation for us as we navigate the path. Right now, it's important to embrace that part of the journey so that we can be real about our starting point and take off. This is about recreating our image; this is exciting stuff we're moving into. Life is waiting for you to fully embrace your true nature and express it outwardly for the benefit of others. Sometimes we feel like we're cursed and that life is out to get us. That thinking serves as a portal for limiting thoughts to come flooding in and take over. When we start to think and feel this way, our energy slides down to low level living, and we struggle to move the needle. Now we have to expand our energy just to try and climb out of this lower level energy. It becomes a vicious cycle of crash, climb, and then crash again. This cyclical pattern of low and high-level energy can be broken. The UN philosophy is our way to overcome it and move the needle toward racing death and fully maximizing our radical pursuit.

THE SEVEN UN MOUNTAINS

I want you to embrace this idea: you are in training, and training requires us to work. This isn't going to happen by osmosis or luck, but it will require energy and the effort on your part to climb the mountains that will build your resiliency and resolve to move your personal needle. I've used these seven mountains myself to achieve my objectives and work toward my Vision.

UN Mountain 1—Reality

If you can't embrace where you're at right now in your life, then you'll struggle with reality. Reality can suck, but it's where you're at. Until you're willing to admit it, you'll never start the needle moving.

UN Mountain 2—Faith

One of the twelve steps in Alcoholics Anonymous is: make a decision to turn our will and our lives over to the care of God as we understood Him. Powerful … and that is the climb we must make on the second mountain. We must be willing to allow God to have a hand in our pursuit and Vision.

UN Mountain 3—Trust

Once we have placed our faith in God, we must trust that His good and perfect will is coded on our heart in our true nature. We must trust ourselves to find His path for us and to do the work of climbing this mountain to continue our journey.

UN Mountain 4—Beginner's Mind

We must take on the mind of a beginner in order to go on this quest. As a beginner, we are open, willing, and can learn quickly. This is the mountain we must climb on the path to mastery. This frees us to learn, grow, and transform.

UN Mountain 5—Kaizen

Kaizen is itself a philosophy. Search the Internet and you'll find copious amounts of information about it. For our purposes, Kaizen is defined as continuous improvement. The key concept of Kaizen is that big results come from small changes and improvements made over time. This is a mountain we climb to help us continually pursue our Vision.

UN Mountain 6—Remarkable

We are extraordinary as we move to the summit and over this mountain. We have etched out our uncommon passion and path for our Vision. Time has allowed us to see our true nature, and we feel worthy of all we have been gifted. Moving is a daily ritual that builds us toward the crescendo of our energy and ability.

UN Mountain 7—Integration

This is where we put it all together into a cohesive unit of living and pursuing. This is a mountain we are climbing continually to live the Vision and be a true-nature pursuer.

SPIRIT GYM

Life is a big gym, and we can train until our heart's content, because our heart's content is the territory of the spirit. Our spirit is the teacher of our class in this gym. We don't approach life with a passive attitude, but we pursue life with abandon and bent on mixing it up with any energy that will stand in our way. We train for all obstacles using the wisdom and knowledge we were gifted when we inherited the Spirit.

We travel through three separate stages on our journey to the promise offered by the cross. It's a lifelong process of training in our spirit gym.

Stage 1—The Beginner

We will spend the most time in on our journey in this stage. To be a beginner is to constantly be open and willing. Never lose this ability and power.

Stage 2—The Warrior

Here we learn to battle through all the obstacles and not lose heart. We don't expect everything to go our way; we know and accept that there will be times they don't go our way. We are disciplined and focused in this stage, willing to sacrifice what isn't necessary for what is.

Stage 3—Mastery
This is the ultimate objective of achieving our Vision and living life based fully on what we know it involves. We will find mastery in different areas of our lives as we journey and integrate all of the lessons we learn into all we do. The ultimate pursuit will always be a continuous quest. We have work to do daily, but we're not put off by what we know will get us to this level of living.

For more information on UN, Spirit Gym, and P–TEAM UNlife coaching, or to hire Daniel as a speaker or for corporate training, visit danieloneill.ca or email Nobody17IM@gmail.com.

FINAL THOUGHTS

Don't you realize that in a race everyone runs,
but only one person gets the prize? So run to win!
All athletes are disciplined in their training. They do it
to win a prize that will fade away, but we do it for an
eternal prize. So I run with purpose in every step. I am
not just shadowboxing. I discipline my body like
an athlete, training it to do what it should.
Otherwise, I fear that after preaching to
others I myself might be disqualified.
(1 Corinthians 9:24–27)

Wow, that's heavy; I'm in the same race as you. I'm on the journey, just as you are. Our paths may differ, and our Visons will be unique. The way you seek mastery will have different objectives than I will. You have a specific coding on your heart that will reflect what you're feeling and seeking to manifest your Vision. Our interests will not carry the same weight as each other's for their own individual pursuit. Your energy will have a different frequency and value than mine, but it's the same race.

I want to make it clear—I am not competing with you, because the prize we seek is the same for all of us. We're all standing at the foot of the cross with an opportunity. We didn't earn this opportunity … it was given to us freely. That's the part of the race we must realize. We're running in this life because of a choice to die made by our Saviour. All the prizes I've won in my athletic career will fade, but the lessons I've learned and pass along to you will not. I run with purpose in every step. I am not perfect, and I will never be. My work toward mastery continues with each step I take. I make those steps with intention and purpose because of the price Christ paid for me to be able to move my needle. All that is radical in me and my pursuit is only possible because I inherited the gift of the Spirit when I chose to be a disciple. The race is real, and I continue to discipline my mind and body so that what I write in this work is not just me being false and asking of others what I am not willing to do myself. With every step I work harder, train harder, pray harder, and believe more in the power of racing death.

Our race is against death, friends. It's against the status quo and the societal conditioning that will deprive us of the ultimate prize. Keep your eye on the real prize. Enjoy the fruits of your labour and the things you earn in life, just don't get lost in these trappings and lose your way in the race to the narrow gate, for on the path there will be those obstacles discussed in here. Your disciplined training will not fail you. The death on the cross will not fail you, and the Coach (God) is more than capable of training you with wisdom and knowledge to achieve success at the end of this race. Our training partner (Spirit) will be with us on all of the lonely runs that feel like a burden but reap the rewards of the discipline. Our redeemer (Jesus) will be cheering for us every step of the way and waiting at the finish line for us. That's a pretty awesome group to train with.

"Breaking the chains of normal and the curse of mediocrity."

ALSO BY DANIEL K. O'NEIL:

Nobody Can Take It Away from You

"Remember to swim at your own pace; don't try to do too much in the water. Save that energy for later in the day. There's the first buoy. I'm a little too far to the left of it, so I'm going to angle to my right a bit and bring myself in closer. I can't believe that this day is here. One year's worth of training and preparation now comes down to this day. Remember to just focus on the swim, dude. You have 2.4 miles in the water—that's all that matters right now. Focus on your stroke, breathe, and relax. Focus on what you're doing, quiet the mind. I sure hope I don't see any big fish—that would be freaky!"

These are the thoughts of a man just after the mass start of the 2004 Ironman Canada Triathlon. They were my thoughts. I had a long day ahead of me, and I was prepared for what was to come. That race is a lot like my life. I am prepared for whatever the world will throw at me, and I have a great mentor who is always with me.